HANGED AT DURHAM

STEVE FIELDING

First published in 2007 by Sutton Publishing Limited

Reprinted in 2008 by
The History Press
The Mill, Brimscombe Port,
Stroud, Gloucestershire, GL5 2QG
www.thehistorypress.co.uk

Reprinted 2009, 2013

British Library Cataloguing in Publication Data
A catalogue record for this book is available from the British Library.

ISBN 978-0-7509-4750-3

Typeset in Goudy.
Typesetting and origination by
Sutton Publishing Limited.
Printed and bound in England.

CONTENTS

ACKNOWLEDGEMENTS

This book would not have been possible but for the help of a number of people. My thanks go to Lisa Moore for help with proofreading and editing the various drafts; to Matthew Spicer for his unselfish help with information and photographs, and for assisting in the many hours of research at The National Archives at Kew; to Tim Leech, who kindly opened his archives and supplied many illustrations and rare documents; to Valerie Robinson at Her Majesty's Prison Durham for help on historical information; to Janet Buckingham for supplying information on a number of cases and for helping with data input and proofreading; and to Stewart Evans for advice on this project.

Finally thanks to the many people who supplied me with a wealth of information and photographs over the years. I have tried to locate the copyright owners of all images used in this book, but a number of them were untraceable. In particular, I have been unable to locate the copyright owner of a number of images sourced from The National Archives. I apologise if I have inadvertently infringed any existing copyright.

Steve Fielding
March 2007
www.stevefielding.com

To be submitted to the High Sheriff

Memorandum of Conditions to which any Person acting as Executioner is required to conform

1. An executioner is engaged and paid by the High Sheriff, and is required to conform with any instructions he may receive from or on behalf of the High Sheriff in connection with any execution for which he may be engaged.

2. A list of persons competent for the office of executioner is in the possession of High Sheriffs and Governors: it is therefore unnecessary for any person to make application for employment in connection with an execution, and such application will be regarded as objectionable conduct and may lead to the removal of the applicant's name from the list.

3. Any person engaged as an executioner will report himself at the prison at which an execution for which he has been engaged is to take place not later than 4 o'clock on the afternoon preceding the day of execution.

4. He is required to remain in the prison from the time of his arrival until the completion of the execution and until permission is given him to leave.

5. During the time he remains in the prison he will be provided with lodging and maintenance on an approved scale.

6. He should avoid attracting public attention in going to or from the prison; he should clearly understand that his conduct and general behaviour must be respectable and discreet, not only at the place and time of execution, but before and subsequently. In particular he must not reveal to any person, whether for publication or not, any information about his work as an Executioner or any information which may come his way in the course of his duty. If he does he will render himself liable to prosecution under the Official Secrets Acts 1911 and 1920.

7. His remuneration will be £10 —— for the performance of the duty required of him, to which will be added £5 —— if his conduct and behaviour have been satisfactory. The latter part of the fee will not be payable until a fortnight after the execution has taken place.

8. Record will be kept of his conduct and efficiency on each occasion of his being employed, and this record will be at the disposal of any High Sheriff who may have to engage an executioner.

9. The name of any person who does not give satisfaction, or whose conduct is in any way objectionable, so as to cast discredit on himself, either in connection with the duties or otherwise, will be removed from the list.

10. The apparatus approved for use at executions will be provided at the prison. No part of it may be removed from the prison, and no apparatus other than approved apparatus must be used in connection with any execution.

11. The executioner will give such information, or make such record of the occurrences as the Governor of the prison may require.

Two copies of these conditions would be sent to the hangman. One would be retained, and the other signed and returned when he accepted an engagement. (Author's collection)

INTRODUCTION

The city of Durham houses one of the most infamous gaols in the country. Notorious residents over the years have included the Kray twins, Myra Hindley, John McVicar, Rose West and Frankie Fraser. It is also the final resting place of almost 100 men and women executed both in public and in private and buried within its walls.

Durham has had a number of gaols built within the city walls over the years and the current prison building is one of the city's best-known landmarks. As is the case today, there were originally two prisons in the city, one being the County Gaol in Saddler Street, the other the old Bridewell or House of Correction built under Elvet Bridge.

The new gaol was commissioned at Old Elvet to replace the earlier one in the Great North Gate, the cause of serious traffic congestion in the city. The Bishop of Durham, Shute Barrington, pledged over £2,000 towards its construction and, on 31 July 1809, Sir Henry Vane Tempest laid the foundation stones. Large crowds gathered to see the bishop place gold, silver and copper coins into the foundations, bands played and soldiers from the Durham militia fired a volley of rifle shots to celebrate the historic occasion.

The gaol at Old Elvet was finally opened for prisoners in 1819, after a building programme that had taken ten years to complete. The project had gone well over budget and resulted in the conviction of the original architect, Francis Sandys, for theft. Sandys, who had also built the nearby Assize court, was incarcerated at the old gaol and his position taken by two architects in succession, the last being famous Durham builder Ignatius Bonomi, who completed the building in April 1819.

Although prisoners were not transferred to the Elvet prison until August 1819, the first execution at the gaol took place three years earlier. On 17 August 1816 John Grieg was hanged for the murder of Elizabeth Stonehouse on a new gallows purposely built outside the courthouse.

The new gaol was comprised of three blocks: to the east were the main prison and House of Correction; running south through the centre was the largest wing, housing male prisoners and a chapel; and to the west was the debtors' prison. There were different rooms for debtors, convicted felons and those still awaiting trial. Little effort was made to segregate inmates; thus those on remand pending trial mixed freely with convicted murderers awaiting either execution or transportation to the colonies.

Conditions at the new gaol were better than those at the Great North Gate, although the prisoner's diet still consisted of two helpings of oatmeal porridge and a pound of bread on Mondays, Wednesdays and Saturdays. On other days it was a few potatoes and fish.

Although there were improvements, the gaol was the subject of several investigations into the treatment and conditions of prisoners. John Howard, a leading prison reform

The new execution shed, built in 1891, housed a scaffold similar to this one from Newgate. (Prison Service Museum)

campaigner, made numerous visits to the gaol, being convinced that the governor was covering up the atrocious conditions prisoners lived in.

Before the 1823 Gaol Act, warders had paid for the right to run the gaol. This allowed them to make money by charging the inmates for items such as food, drinking water and 'other services' provided. This included the releasing prisoners at their discretion, providing straw for bedding, allowing prostitutes to visit, and the selling of alcohol.

The new Act reflected the changes in attitude to punishment and criminals. Now male and female prisoners were segregated, as were debtors and felons. New rules forbade drinking, swearing and blasphemy, disobedience and indecent behaviour, and prisoners were now classified and separated according to their crimes. Many were put to work: minor offenders had tasks such as clearing rubbish and gardening, while long-term prisoners were often employed in the oakum-picking workshops.

The gaol also had a variety of punishments. These varied according to the misdemeanour but included flogging, birching, the crank, the treadmill and solitary confinement. The treadmill was used as a punishment when an inmate had severely broken the prison rules. They were made to turn the treadmill by walking on it for hours on end at a certain pace determined by warders. Another type of punishment was the crank: prisoners were made to turn a machine with a metal handle resembling a car's starting handle, which served no purpose whatsoever. As the prisoner gradually became accustomed to the force needed to turn the handle, warders adjusted a tension screw, thereby making it more difficult to turn. This is said to be the reason prison officers are known to this day as 'screws'.

Before the building of the new gaol, executions were held at the site of the old Dryburn Hospital (to the north of Durham city) and a small metal plaque still marks the spot where they were carried out. Accounts of the origins of the name Dryburn are mixed: one story is that a Jesuit priest was hanged there and, after his death, the adjacent stream (burn) dried up and never flowed again. It may also be a corruption of the name Tyburn, the name of London's infamous site of execution dating from the Middle Ages to late into the eighteenth century.

Executions at Durham, as at many other towns and cities, were popular spectator events, with crowds often numbering into the thousands travelling from all parts of the county to witness the condemned pay the penalty. Executioners of the day needed no special skills, and often had little or no experience before being entrusted with carrying out an execution.

In 1780, Bartholomew Pendleton acquired the office of executioner by virtue of being related to the Canon of Durham Cathedral. His inexperience led to a bungled execution when he overestimated the length of drop required, and the ensuing long drop resulted in decapitation of the condemned man. Pendleton's payment was withheld as a result of the error and for future executions he used a much shorter drop. This resulted in death by painful strangulation, with the criminal squirming and choking on the end of the rope for anything up to half an hour, instead of a swift death from a broken neck.

The last execution at Dryburn was that of Richard Metcalfe, hanged on 12 August 1805 for the murder of his son-in-law. Murder was not the only crime punishable by death and, on 12 April 1819, George Atcheson was hanged for the rape of a 10-year-old girl, three years before the only other execution for rape, of miner Henry Anderson, on 12 March 1822.

Other notable public executions include that of Thomas Clarke, a 19-year-old domestic servant at Hallgarth Mill, who was convicted of the murder of 17-year-old housemaid Mary Ann Westhorpe. Clark was sentenced to death by hanging, and afterwards his body was to be handed over to surgeons for dissection. The execution took place at midday on Monday 28 February 1831, before a crowd estimated at more than 15,000. Thomas claimed on the gallows: 'Gentlemen, I die for another man's crimes. I am innocent.'

In 1832, William Jobling was wrongly convicted of the murder of Nicholas Fairles, a local magistrate, near Jarrow Slake. Following public protests over the conditions in the South Shields workhouse, supported by strikes by the local miners, the authorities sent in soldiers to quell the disturbances. As the militia tried to evict striking miners, a policeman was killed. The actual killer absconded but Jobling, who had been present and had done nothing to help, was judged to be equally guilty and made a scapegoat. Over 100 mounted hussars and infantrymen were positioned in front of the goal as Jobling was led to the gallows and hanged.

As a warning to others, his body was gibbeted after death. After hanging for the customary hour, it was removed from the rope, stripped and dipped in molten tar to preserve it. It was then dressed in the clothes he had been hanged in, loaded into a cart and paraded around the town before being taken to the scene of the murder. Placed in

Particulars of the condemned Prisoner	Particulars of the Execution
Name: Frank Stokes.	The length of the drop as determined before the execution: 6 feet 11 inches
Register Number: 1418.	The length of the drop, as measured after the execution, from the level of the floor of the scaffold to the heels of the suspended culprit: 7 feet 1 inches
Sex: male.	Cause of death [(a) Dislocation of vertebræ, (b) Asphyxia]: Dislocation of cervical vertebrae
Age: 44 years.	Approximate statement of the character and amount of destruction to the soft and bony structures of the neck: Fracture dislocation of cervical vertebrae, tearing and stretching of soft tissues
Height: 5' 5½"	If there were any peculiarities in the build or condition of the prisoner, or in the structure of his neck, which necessitated a departure from the scale of drops, particulars should be stated: none
Build: Prop.	
Weight in clothing (to be taken on the day preceding the execution): 162 lbs	
Character of the prisoner's neck: Proportinate	

Records respecting the Executioner and his Assistants (if any).

	Name and Address, in full, of the Executioner.	Name and Address, in full, of the 1st Assistant to the Executioner (if any).	Name and Address, in full, of the 2nd Assistant to the Executioner (if any).
	Harry Bernard Allen, Junction Hotel, Whitefield, near Manchester.	Harry Smith, 86 Cantley Avenue, Cantley Estate, Doncaster.	

Opinion of the Governor and Medical Officer as to the manner in which each of the above-named persons has performed his duty.

	Executioner	1st Assistant	2nd Assistant
1. Has he performed his duty satisfactorily?	1. Yes	1. YES	1.
2. Was his general demeanour satisfactory during the period that he was in the prison, and does he appear to be a respectable person?	2. Yes	2. YES	2.
3. Has he shown capacity, both physical and mental, for the duty, and general suitability for the post?	3. Yes	3. YES	3.
4. Is there any ground for supposing that he will bring discredit upon his office by lecturing, or by granting interviews to persons who may seek to elicit information from him in regard to the execution or by any other act?	4. No	4. No	4.
5. Are you aware of any circumstances occurring before, at, or after the execution which tend to show that he is not a suitable person to employ on future occasions either on account of incapacity for performing the duty, or the likelihood of his creating public scandal before or after an execution?	5. No	5. No.	5.

4/9/58

Following an execution, all the data were recorded on an official LPC4 sheet. (Author's collection)

a gibbet cage of flat bars of iron, Jobling was suspended and left as a frightening warning of the consequences of crime. His friends later snatched the body and gave him a proper burial.

With the opening of the new gaol, a new type of gallows was erected on the steps outside the new courthouse. Holes to house the beams that supported the platform are still visible in the wall. Following conviction at the Assizes, the prisoner was brought from the adjacent courthouse to the prison through an internal passage and led out for the execution through a passage fashioned from a window, on to the platform of the gallows set up over the main entrance. This was the usual arrangement in many gaols. It was simpler and safer than escorting the prisoner out of the main gates and making him climb the steps to the gallows. Houses across the street with views of the drop would rent out their balconies to those who could afford to pay for the best view of an execution.

The last public execution in Durham was that of Matthew Atkinson on 16 March 1865, hanged for wife-murder at Spen near Winlaton. Thomas Askern was the executioner and the rope broke when Atkinson was placed on the gallows and the lever pulled. The condemned man crashed to the floor and, after being revived, was able to talk with witnesses while a new rope was sought. Thirty minutes later, Atkinson was hanged at the second attempt.

After the abolition of public hangings in 1868, the gallows was set up in the condemned prisoners' exercise yard in the gaol. The platform was on level ground, fixed over a brick-lined pit. In 1890, a purpose-built execution shed was constructed and used for the first time a year later. Again it was outside in the grounds. This was standard practice at all prisons, but still required the prisoner to make a long walk from the condemned cell, in the case of Durham, on A Wing. The execution shed often had more than one purpose and, at Durham, it also accommodated the prison van.

By the middle of the twentieth century, Durham had a permanent gallows, built to the standard Home Office pattern and housed at the end of D Wing. Built in 1925, this new area had two condemned cells, one adjacent to the gallows, the other separated from the execution chamber by the corridor, which led to the exercise yard. The condemned cells were usually constructed by knocking two or sometimes three standard cells into one. They contained a toilet and washbasin and sometimes had a small alcove, which was converted into an interview area for visitors.

There was a lobby between the cell and the execution chamber, and a mortuary in the yard adjoining the ground floor of the execution chamber. Parts of the execution block remain to this day, although the condemned cell has been removed and the pit covered over. Now used for storage, this area was later renamed E Wing.

Like many old gaols, Durham is reputed to have a ghost. In December 1947, 23-year-old inmate John Slater stabbed to death a fellow prisoner, Norman Eaton, with a table knife. In February 1948, he was sentenced to death and moved to the condemned cell at Durham. Slater was later found insane and transferred to Broadmoor. Shortly after the murder, another prisoner was placed in the cell where the murder took place. The following morning he was found crouched in the corner, stricken with terror. He told the warders he had witnessed a ghostly re-enactment of the murder. When other prisoners also objected to being locked up in the cell, claiming they had seen a ghost, it was converted into a storeroom.

In total, ninety-two men and two women were hanged at Durham between 1800 and 1958. Ninety-one of these executions took place at the prison and three at Dryburn. Seventeen were in public. Only four convicts were executed for crimes other than murder. A complete list of latter-day executions at Durham is included in the appendices to this book.

All of those executed in the last century were buried alongside the prison hospital wall, with only the date of execution and a broad arrow carved into the wall to mark the location of their grave. With just a prison-issue shirt as a shroud, the body was placed into a thin pine box and covered with quicklime. Numerous holes were bored into the box before burial, to help speed up decomposition.

In the early 1990s, as the gaol was being modernised, the graves of some of those executed, including Mary Cotton, were disturbed. Workmen found a pair of women's shoes attached to her skeletal frame. The bodies were removed from the gaol and later cremated.

Durham Gaol did not retain its own hangman, and instead called upon the services of the country's chief executioner. The first to officiate at Durham following the abolition of public executions was William Calcraft. Calcraft may have previously visited the city carrying out public executions, but it was Yorkshireman Thomas Askern who performed the majority of latter-day public hangings, including the bungled hanging of Atkinson in the last public execution at the gaol. When Calcraft was finally pensioned off, William Marwood took his place. Marwood's own career was not without incident, and ended with the terrible events at the execution of James Burton as recorded in Chapter 16.

Victorian hangmen Bartholomew Binns, James Berry and James Billington were all visitors to the gaol and, following Billington's death, two of his sons, William and John, carried out executions here. The name probably most associated with executions in the twentieth century is that of Pierrepoint, and the first of that name to officiate at Durham was Manchester furniture salesman Henry Pierrepoint. The first of Henry's five visits to the gaol was for the double execution of Noble and Lawman in 1908. On his first three trips to Durham, he was accompanied by his older brother Thomas as his assistant.

Rochdale barber John Ellis had first visited the gaol as assistant to John Billington at the execution of George Breeze in 1904, and acted as chief executioner at four executions between 1914 and 1920. In November 1920, Ellis had to refuse the offer to hang James Riley, as he had already accepted an engagement at Exeter. The offer was then made to Tom Pierrepoint, who accepted and was present at every subsequent hanging here until 1946, a total of twenty-six executions, including two doubles.

In March 1946, Stephen Wade was engaged to carry out an execution, despite never having visited the gaol as an assistant, and never before having officiated at an execution as a 'number one' at any gaol. This appointment of a novice was an unusual step, as the man who had succeeded Tom Pierrepoint was his nephew Albert Pierrepoint. The son of Henry Pierrepoint, Albert was destined to become the best-known hangman of modern times following his executions of notorious killers such as John Christie, Derek Bentley and Ruth Ellis. Despite being the chief executioner for fifteen years, Pierrepoint was to make just one visit to Durham as chief, in 1950, when Wade was unable to officiate through illness.

Wade performed his debut execution to everyone's satisfaction, and officiated at six of the seven executions in the period leading up to 1956, when hanging was temporarily halted during a Parliamentary debate. Wade died in December 1956 and was replaced on the short Home Office list of executioners by Harry Allen, who had been the assistant at his first execution in 1946.

Allen was the chief executioner at the hanging of John Willson Vickers in 1957. It was also his debut as chief executioner, having succeeded Albert Pierrepoint in the previous year. It was the first execution in Great Britain in almost two years, and the first to be sanctioned under the new Homicide Act. Allen was also engaged for the execution of Frank Stokes in September 1958 but had to reject the offer to hang Brian Chandler a few months later, as he was due in Cyprus on official business.

Robert Leslie 'Jock' Stewart carried out the execution of Chandler in what turned out to be the last execution at the gaol. Chandler was the last occupant of the condemned cell, which was dismantled following the abolition of capital punishment in the late 1960s.

This book looks in detail at the stories behind the seventy-five murder cases that led to the killers' being *Hanged at Durham* following the passing of the Private Execution Act of 1868.

1

A FATAL DECISION

❖ *John Dolan, 22 March 1869* ❖

Catherine Keeshan ran a lodging house on Union Lane, Sunderland. She shared the house with her lover of the previous three years, 37-year-old Irish labourer John Dolan, and two lodgers, Hugh Ward and Edward Collins. Ward had taken lodgings there in October 1868 and seemed initially to be on good terms with Dolan.

On 8 December, Dolan and Ward went out drinking, and during the night their discussion turned to Dolan's paramour, with Ward apparently making some comment about Catherine to which Dolan took exception. They returned to the house in the early hours and Dolan gave Catherine money to go out and buy some ale. When she returned, Ward poured himself a drink but Dolan refused, saying he had to be up early for work on the following morning. Ward then poured a glass for the woman, at which point Dolan jumped to his feet and dragged Catherine out of the room.

They went to their bedroom, where her screams brought Ward running to the room. Dolan pacified him, saying he would not cause any more trouble and Ward went back to his drink. Moments later, more screams rang out and Ward returned to the room and began to fight with Dolan.

Catherine rushed out to find a policeman and in the company of four constables she returned to the house, whereupon the situation calmed down. No sooner had the police departed than Dolan locked the door behind them and started causing trouble. Catherine jumped through the window and called for the police to return, asking them to arrest her drunken lover. They again warned Dolan, who was clearly drunk and aggressive, about his conduct and when Dolan lunged at the woman, he was restrained and hit twice by a policeman. Still they refused to take him into custody, despite her pleas. It was a fatal decision that was to cost two men their lives.

Hangman William Calcraft officiated at the first private executions at Durham. (Crime Picture Archive)

The police finally left the house after Dolan told them he was going to bed, but as Catherine watched him go upstairs she sensed it was not the end of the matter. Following him to the bedroom she could see he was rummaging through a bag. She knew he kept a shoemaker's knife in it and shouted to Ward to watch out. She rushed out to find the police but before they could return Dolan had viciously stabbed Ward in the stomach and face. The first wound tore open his stomach, the second blinded him in the left eye. Ward died from his injuries a few days later.

Dolan was tried before Mr Justice Lush at Durham Assizes on 24 February 1869; his defence was manslaughter through provocation. The jury took just minutes to find that there was no provocation for a brutal attack and return a verdict of guilty of wilful murder.

2

THE DARLINGTON FENIAN MURDER

❖ *John McConville, 22 March 1869* ❖

Late on the night of Saturday 30 January 1869, Philip Trainer, an Irish labourer, entered the Allan Arms at Darlington. He stayed for twenty minutes, but no sooner had he left the building than a shot rang out. When witnesses went outside they found him lying in a pool of blood in the adjacent alleyway. He had been shot in the left eye, the bullet penetrating the brain and killing him instantly.

The police were called and, arriving at the public house, they found that although several people had apparently witnessed the attack, nobody was talking. Following several days of enquiries, police eventually arrested John McConville, a 23-year-old Irish furnace puddler, on suspicion of being involved. He denied shooting Trainer but police soon gained enough evidence to charge him with murder.

At his trial before Mr Justice Lush, it was learned that Trainer had previously been a member of a Fenian gang but had begun to distance himself from their subversive activities to the extent that he announced he was leaving the society. On the night of his murder he had gone into the pub for a drink and happened across several members of the gang already drinking there. A scuffle broke out, at which the landlord asked them to leave and it was at this point that McConville had taken out his pistol and fatally wounded Trainer.

Following the conviction, it was announced that the prisoner had a long history of offences through his involvement with the Fenian movement. He had served terms of imprisonment for his proclivities and sympathies and had been involved in the infamous attack on a police van in Manchester that had led to the murder of a policeman and the execution of three men at Salford.

McConville was hanged alongside John Dolan in the first private executions carried out at Durham. It was only the fifth execution carried out in England since the Capital Punishment Amendment Act of 1868, abolishing public executions. It was also the first double execution. William Calcraft officiated, having made the long journey by train from his home near London.

3

HANGED SIDE BY SIDE

❖ *John Hayes and Hugh Slane, 13 January 1873* ❖

Four years after the first double execution carried out inside Durham Gaol, two more men also shared the gallows. This was to be one of the rare occasions when two prisoners simultaneously paid the ultimate penalty for the same crime.

It was late on the evening of Saturday 16 November 1872, and at their home that doubled as a tobacconist's shop on Duncombe Street, Spennymoor, Jane and Joseph Waine prepared to settle down for the night. There was a knock at the back door and in walked next-door neighbour, 22-year-old Hugh Slane, who asked to purchase some matches. What happened next led to the trial of four men for murder.

Slane noticed the Waines' lodger, John Wilson, sitting by the fire in the kitchen. He asked Wilson if he had been in Carrick's Beerhouse earlier, where there had been some trouble. Wilson said he was a stranger to the area, that he had no money and he did not know where the beer house was. Slane called him a liar and the two men squared up, only to be separated by Joseph Waine, who ushered his neighbour out into the back alley.

Waine ignored Slane's requests to come outside and fight, and instead he leisurely took out his pipe and went to the door to smoke it. A few minutes later, as Waine was talking to his 12-year-old son, Isaac, Slane reappeared, threw the contents of the matchbox into Waine's face and grabbed him by the lapels. As they stumbled into the alley, Slane whistled a signal and three men appeared from around the corner and proceeded to kick and batter Waine senseless. As his wife rushed to find a policeman, Wilson and Waine's son helped the shopkeeper back into the kitchen. A neighbour went to fetch a doctor but, although Waine received prompt medical attention, he succumbed to his injuries and died later that night.

Police soon had four men in custody: Hugh Slane, 29-year-old John Hayes, 19-year-old Terence Rice and 27-year-old George Beesley. They were remanded to appear before Mr Justice Denham at Durham Assizes in December. The evidence of Isaac Waine, who testified that Slane had called for the help of his friends by whistling for them to join the fight, suggested premeditation. It was a short trial, the jury taking a matter of minutes to find all four guilty as charged. They were sentenced to death and the date of execution was fixed for 6 January 1873.

Petitions for clemency were gathered and sent to the Home Secretary but, although the original date of execution was put back a week, there was no suggestion that a reprieve for any would be forthcoming. Just when it seemed that all four would face the hangman, word came through thirty-six hours before the appointed time that Rice and Beesley had had their sentences commuted to life imprisonment. Slane and Hayes were left to face the hangman. They were hanged side by side.

4

THE FIRST FEMALE SERIAL KILLER

❖ *Mary Ann Cotton, 24 March 1873* ❖

Mary Ann Cotton – she's dead and she's rotten,
She lies in her bed – with her eyes wide open.
Sing, sing! Oh, what can I sing?
Mary Ann Cotton is tied up with string.
Where, where? Up in the air,
Selling black puddings a penny a pair.

(Popular Victorian children's rhyme)

Charles Cotton passed away suddenly. On 12 July 1872, his stepmother, Mary Ann Cotton, told the doctor that the 7-year-old had died from gastric fever, but both the doctor and her neighbours were suspicious. Other members of the family had died by similar stomach ailments in recent months, and soon gossip and suspicion spread like wildfire through West Auckland. When it reached the attention of the police, they began an investigation and looked into the background of 40-year-old Mrs Cotton.

Born Mary Ann Robson in the village of Low Moorsley in October of 1832, she had an unhappy childhood. She left home at 16, then gave up her job as a domestic servant in South Hetton when she fell pregnant to her first husband, William Mowbray. During the first five years of their marriage they travelled the country, with Mary giving birth to five children, four of whom died in infancy.

In January 1865, William Mowbray was injured at sea and returned to their home in Sunderland to nurse his swollen foot. A few weeks later, despite a doctor's care, he died from a sudden intestinal disorder. Soon after Mowbray's death, Mary moved to Seaham Harbour, where she struck up a relationship with Joseph Nattrass, a local man who was engaged to another woman. Here, another child died, the eighth to meet that fate of the nine to whom she had given birth.

The last home of Mary Cotton at West Auckland. (Crime Picture Archive)

Mary returned to Sunderland and found employment at a local infirmary, while her sole surviving child went to live with her grandmother. At Sunderland Infirmary, she began courting a patient and, soon after he was discharged, they married at Monkwearmouth in August 1865. He soon developed health problems and died in October 1866 after chronic stomach problems. Although it was her second case of widowhood in two years, it seemed that no one was suspicious of the hard-working nurse.

In November 1866, Mary answered an advertisement placed by recently widowed shipwright James Robinson. He needed a housekeeper to look after his children and to maintain the house. Shortly before Christmas, the youngest child developed gastric fever and died. Overcome with grief, James turned to Mary for comfort and she was soon pregnant with his child.

In March 1867, Mary's mother fell ill and she moved in to nurse her. Soon, her mother began complaining of stomach pains and died nine days later. Mary's daughter Isabella came back to live with her and, on returning to the Robinson house, she too soon developed a debilitating stomach ailment. Robinson's two older children were also taken ill and by the end of April all three were dead. The grief-stricken Robinson did not suspect his wife-to-be and they married in August. Their first child, Mary Isabella, was born in November, but on 1 March 1868, she too succumbed to illness.

Robinson had by now become suspicious of his wife and threw her out of the house. Besides the tragic sudden deaths of the children, debts were building up. There was also the matter of her constant requests for him to insure his life.

In 1870, a friend introduced Mary to her brother, Frederick Cotton. They married in September and Mary quickly insured the lives of her new husband and his two sons. She gave birth to a son in early 1871 and, when she learned that Joseph Nattrass was now living

Mary Ann Cotton as depicted in the Illustrated Police News. (Crime Picture Archive)

in nearby West Auckland, she moved the family there and rekindled the relationship.

In December 1871 Frederick Cotton died of gastric fever and Nattrass began to lodge at Mary's house. Mary had also found work as a nurse to John Quick-Manning, a customs officer who was recovering from smallpox. Mary soon became pregnant by him and decided that he was to be husband number four. Realising that marriage to Quick-Manning was hampered by the remaining members of the Cotton household, she went to work and, by the summer of 1872, both children were dead. Nattrass passed away soon after the last child, and also shortly after changing his will, leaving everything to Mary Cotton.

Shortly before Charles Cotton's death, Mary had spoken to Thomas Riley, a local-government official, about the possibility of sending him into a workhouse. Informed that it would only be possible if she went with him, she coldly told Riley that the boy was in the way of a marriage with Quick-Manning, and '. . . he'll go like all the rest of the Cotton family.'

When he learned of the child's death, Riley spoke to a doctor and outlined his suspicions. The doctor was surprised to hear of the news, as he had tended to Charles several times during the previous week and had detected nothing life-threatening. The doctor delayed issuing a death certificate until an investigation could take place.

Instead of calling on the doctor after the boy's death, Mary visited the office of the insurance company to collect on the policy. Learning that money could not be released until she presented a death certificate, she called to see the doctor. Mary was told she could not have a signed death certificate until a formal inquest had been held.

The subsequent inquest found that death was not due to natural causes. When the story was picked up on by local newspapers, resentment toward her in West Auckland quickly built up. Appalled by the gossip, Quick-Manning severed all contact with Mary, who made plans to leave the area.

Samples of Charles's stomach contents were analysed and tested positive for arsenic. The doctor contacted the police, who arrested Mary and ordered the bodies of both Charles and Joseph Nattrass be exhumed. Both tested positive for the presence of arsenic. Although officers built up a long list of suspicious deaths, it was decided to proceed with the single murder charge of Charles Cotton. Mary was heavily pregnant at the time and, once she had given birth, the trial began.

County Gaol. Durham
7th March 1873

Sir,

I beg to inform you that at the Assizes holden in Durham on Friday the 7th day of March 1873. Mary Ann Cotton was convicted of Wilful Murder and sentenced to be hanged, consequently in accordance with the Rules laid down in your Order dated 13th August 1868. Mary Ann Cotton will be executed on Monday the 24th Inst. at 8 o'clock Am.

I have the honor, to be
Sir.
Your Most Obedt Servant
[illegible]
Lt Colonel
Governor

The Right Hon. H. A. Bruce
Secretary of State
Home Department
Whitehall

Letter informing the Home Secretary of the date fixed for the execution of Mary Ann Cotton. (Crime Picture Archive)

The court heard of the long list of gastric fever victims and about Mary's statements describing Charles as an obstacle towards marriage, and numerous witnesses testified to her purchases of arsenic. The defence claimed that Charles could have inhaled loose airborne particles of arsenic, as it was used as a dye in the green wallpaper of the Cotton home.

Mr Justice Archibald in his summing-up dismissed this theory and the jury retired for just ninety minutes before returning to find Mary guilty of murder. She continued to protest her innocence and had to be carried from the dock after collapsing on hearing the verdict.

Mary Ann Cotton. (Author's collection)

On 24 March 1873, she was led to the scaffold erected in the courtyard, where veteran hangman William Calcraft placed the noose around her neck and pulled the lever. The trapdoors opened and she dropped into the pit. But death was not instant: she struggled slowly and painfully on the end of the rope for over three minutes before life was extinct.

Mary Ann Cotton holds a place in the annals of crime as one of the most notorious poisoners on record. In her greed and the desire to rid herself of people who became obstacles in her life, the total number of victims in her twenty-year killing spree could be as many as twenty-one. Her death count was surpassed only by mass murderer Dr Harold Shipman, who also spent time in a Durham prison cell a century and quarter later.

5

AN UNCONTROLLABLE TEMPER

❖ Charles Dawson, 5 January 1874 ❖

In the late summer of 1873, four men went out drinking in Darlington. They were Charles Dawson, who shared a house with Martha Addison at Cleveland Street, Darlington, along with their three lodgers, Tom Mullen, Pat Dempsey and John Harper. Dawson and Mrs Addison had been living together for two years, since he left his wife at Stockton and moved in with her.

Apart from the money from their tenants, both made a small income, hers legitimately from selling home-made ginger beer to the ironworkers at the factory across from her home; Dawson earned some of his money from labouring work in the ironworks, but most of it from poaching. It was well known that he was a violent man and often lost his temper with Mrs Addison, usually when drunk.

On the evening of Saturday 13 September, the men visited a number of public houses, where Dawson told Mullen he was going to find Martha, with whom he had had a quarrel earlier in the evening. They parted and Dawson soon found Martha walking near a railway cutting at Albert Hill. They exchanged words and he struck her in the face, knocking her to the floor. He then helped her to her feet and they returned home, where Mullen was sitting drinking in the kitchen.

Dawson's temper had now become uncontrollable. He locked the door and threatened Mullen that he would kill him if he told police about what he was going to see. At that, he picked up Mullen's beer bottle and hit Martha across the head, knocking her to the floor. He then kicked her several times before jumping up and down on her as she lay motionless on the floor. He finished the murderous assault by striking her in the face with a heavy cooking dish, knocking several teeth out.

Perhaps realising the seriousness of his actions, Dawson began to sponge away the blood from the stricken woman, but it was too late: Martha was mortally wounded and beyond help. Minutes later, lodger Dempsey arrived home and unlocked the door. Mullen seized the opportunity to flee, hurrying to fetch a policeman. Dawson was taken into custody later that night. Cause of death was found to be from the head injury caused by the initial blow from the bottle.

There could be no defence to such a brutal crime, and the lodger's eyewitness account that the attack was unprovoked destroyed any hope of a defence of manslaughter or provocation. At Durham Assizes on 11 December, Mr Justice Honyman sentenced Dawson to death, agreeing fully with the jury's verdict.

6

A SMALL BOTTLE OF PORTER

❖ *Edward Gough, 5 January 1874* ❖

Mr Justice Honyman's sitting at Durham's Winter Assizes in December 1873 was a busy one. Five murder cases were heard in three days, the third of which was the case of the wilful murder of James Partridge at Sunnyside, County Durham.

On 7 July 1873, Edward Gough, a pitman, called into a pub at Sunnyside and ordered a glass of porter. Also in the bar was James Partridge, another pitman, who was drinking with a group of friends. Partridge told Gough not to buy such a small drink: 'What's the use of ordering a small bottle of porter? Why don't you order something we can all share?' Gough ignored Partridge's mocking tone and, finishing his drink, he left quietly, while Partridge and his friends carried on drinking and laughing.

Gough did not intend to let the incident rest though. He returned home and confided in a friend what had happened. They agreed to go back to the pub to confront Partridge, and as they went out of the door, Gough slipped a knife into his jacket pocket.

Returning to the public house, Gough approached Partridge and challenged him to a fight. After a few minutes of pushing and shoving, they made their way to the door and, as Partridge made to remove his jacket, Gough lunged at him, knife in hand. Partridge recoiled in shock and pain and, seeing his adversary was holding a knife, he began to run away, with Gough in pursuit. Moments later, with blood oozing from a deep wound, Partridge fell to the ground. He died a short time later.

At his trial, Gough pleaded guilty to manslaughter through provocation but, although there was evidence that Partridge had mocked him in the bar earlier, there was not the provocation there to justify Gough's returning with a knife. Witnesses testified that Gough had lunged at Partridge as he was unable to defend himself while removing his coat, and that there was no provocation other than his agreeing to Gough's request for a fight. Returning a guilty verdict, the jury added a recommendation for mercy, considering the excitement the prisoner was under at the time of the murder.

7

FOR HER LOVE . . .

❖ *William Thompson, 5 January 1874* ❖

For Jane Atchison, it was second time unlucky. Her first marriage had not been a happy one and, shortly after the birth of her child, she left her husband and went to stay with relatives at Felling, near Newcastle. Here she met William Thompson and, although her relatives warned her against rushing into another marriage, she ignored their advice and went ahead with her plans. This time, however, it was a bigamous marriage: she had not completed divorce proceedings from her first husband when she pledged her troth to Thompson at Gateshead Register Office in February 1872. She was just 19 at the time, her new husband being five years older.

This marriage also soon deteriorated, and less than a year later she was back at her father's home. Thompson discovered where she was living and, although her father had been against the marriage at first, he thought Thompson was genuinely trying to salvage the relationship and allowed his son-in-law to stay at the house at Annfield Plain while they worked at the marriage.

All seemed fine until Saturday 4 October 1873, when Thompson and his wife spent the day in Newcastle. At lunchtime they went for a meal in a local public house and, after they had eaten, Jane spotted a group of men, one of whom was her cousin, and went to join them, leaving Thompson sitting alone. He seethed at this and was overheard saying to Jane: 'Wait till we get home . . . it will be you or me for it!' They shared a carriage back home with two women who overheard him making threats concerning what he would do to her when they returned home.

They arrived at 7 p.m. and as Jane prepared supper she asked her father to fetch some beer from a local pub. Alone at last with his wife, Thompson began to berate her for her earlier conduct. What happened next was contested at his trial, but moments later Jane Thompson ran out of the house screaming and clutching her throat. She reached the home of a friend two doors away, where she collapsed and died. Thompson had by this time fled from the house and was arrested at his brother's house at Dipton later that night.

His defence was that during the quarrel she had cut her own throat during a struggle, but this was quickly shown to be false when the police surgeon who examined the body found that the throat wound was so severe only the spinal cord had prevented decapitation. This clearly ruled out suicide and when the testimonies of the women who had shared the carriage from Newcastle were heard in the court, the verdict was a formality.

Thompson was hanged alongside the two other men convicted at the same assizes, Edward Gough and Charles Dawson. The prison chaplain attended to the men, except for Gough, who as a Catholic was visited by the Revd Canon Consitt. On Sunday night, 4 January 1874, each retired for the night at 10 p.m. and, apart from Gough, who had a fretful night, the others slept soundly until roused by warders. After a light breakfast they were moved to the press room at 7.45 a.m., where executioner Marwood pinioned the prisoners and the procession to the scaffold formed.

As they left the press room, Thompson called out, 'I die for her love.' When they reached the scaffold, Thompson was placed in the centre on the trapdoors, with Dawson to his left, Gough to his right. At 8.08 a.m. all was ready and Marwood pulled the lever. Gough and Dawson died instantly. In Thompson's case, death eventually came after a terrible struggle on the end of the rope. Over a hundred people gathered at the prison gates to watch the black flag hoisted to show that the three killers had paid for their crimes.

8

A QUESTION OF PROVOCATION

❖ Hugh Daley, 28 December 1874 ❖

Irish-born Hugh Daley worked as a cinder-drawer at a pit close to his home at High Bush Blades, near Dinton, a few miles from Consett. On 7 November 1874, he and a friend had been out drinking in a number of public houses, and by closing time he was very drunk.

They returned to Daley's home, where they found another Irish pitman, Philip Burdey, asleep inside his house.

Daley ordered Burdey out of the house but the man was seemingly so drunk he was unable to understand the orders. A few minutes later, Daley picked up a poker and began to hit the helpless Burdey with it. As Daley struck the blows, he ordered his wife to go and fetch a policeman to shift the man from the house.

She returned an hour later in the company of a policeman, by which time Daley had been raining blows on Burdey, who by now he had managed to drag into the front street, for over an hour. Placed under arrest, Daley was conveyed to the local police station while Burdey was taken back inside and examined by a doctor, but he died a short time later. At the inquest it was found that almost every bone in Burdey's head and upper body was shattered.

Daley was tried before Mr Justice Baron Cleasby on 11 December at Durham Assizes. His counsel admitted that the death of Burdey had been caused by the violence of the prisoner, but argued that he had not acted with the intention of taking his life. Upon coming home and finding the trespasser in his house, Daley had acted as he did with the intention of throwing him out, but his condition of frenzied drunkenness rendered him incapable of any intent to kill.

Summing up the case, the judge asked the jury to consider whether there was any question of provocation that could reduce the charge to manslaughter, or if they believed the prisoner was guilty as charged of murder. They were warned that the prisoner's drunken state was no excuse for the attack.

After considering a verdict for an hour and a half, they found the prisoner guilty of murder but added a strong recommendation for mercy on account of the great provocation the prisoner had suffered in finding the deceased in his house. The judge warned the prisoner not to hope that the sentence would not be carried out, although he would forward the recommendation to the proper quarters.

9

MURDER ON EASTER SUNDAY

❖ Michael Gilligan, 2 August 1875 ❖

On 8 July 1875, three men stood in the dock at Durham Assizes before Mr Justice Baron Huddlestone, accused of a brutal murder. Michael Gilligan, James Durkin and James Flynn were charged with the wilful murder of John Kilcran, a 42-year-old Irish labourer, at Darlington on 28 March last.

On Easter Sunday night, Kilcran and a friend had been drinking in the Lord Nelson Inn. When they had finished their drinks, Kilcran walked his friend home before setting off for his own home. As he made his way back towards the Lord Nelson, he ran into a gang of six youths who seemed to be searching for someone. As they passed the Malt Shovel public house, Durkin looked inside then returned, telling his friends, 'He's not in there!'

Moments later, they reached a crossroads at the same moment that Kilcran approached, unsteady on his feet and clearly the worse for drink. Without warning and for no apparent reason, one of the men punched him several times in the face. Gilligan then reached into his pocket and pulled out a chisel, which he hurled with great force at the Irishman, striking him on the forehead and making a noise like the sound of a gun being fired, heard by witnesses 60 yards down the road.

Kilcran was carried home, where it was found he had a fracture in his skull almost 3in across. He was able to give descriptions of his attackers to the police and, within a short time, three of the men were taken into custody, charged with assault. Ten days later, the charge was changed to one of murder when Kilcran died from his injuries.

Gilligan, 22 years old and described as a respectable young man, argued that it was a case of mistaken identity and it was not his hand that had caused the fatal injuries, but numerous witnesses came forward alleging he had led the assault.

Returning their verdict, the jury found Durkin and Flynn guilty of manslaughter and they were sentenced to fifteen years' imprisonment; Gilligan they found guilty of murder. Following the passing of the sentence, the condemned man made a long statement, protesting that he had not been party to the killing, adding that if his companions were honest men they would say so.

10

THE BODY IN THE RIVER

❖ *William McHugh, 2 August 1875* ❖

When the body of a man was pulled from the River Tees at Barnard Castle on Sunday morning, 11 March 1875, it was initially thought that death was due to drowning. He would not have been the first drunk to stumble into the murky river and drown. However, when the body was removed to the mortuary, the police surgeon informed officers that this was not a simple drowning, but was probably a case of murder.

It was found that the body, identified as that of Thomas Mooney, had wounds above the eye and, although the cause of death was drowning, it seemed likely he had been beaten up before he was thrown into the water. As police began investigating the suspicious death, witnesses came forward claiming they had heard two men discussing the death of Mooney while drinking in Dobson's Beerhouse. Police soon had four men in custody and pieced together the events leading up to the discovery of the body.

Mooney was an Irish labourer who was separated from his wife and child. On Saturday 10 April, he had gone to a house at Bridgegate to visit his child, and later, after a night out visiting a number of public houses, he had returned to an adjacent house where a group of Irishmen had gathered. In the course of the night an argument broke out, during which Mooney received a blow to the head. Later, two men had left to find lodgings but, failing to do so, returned to the house in time to see Mooney being dragged along a passage that led to the river by a pair of individuals identified as William McHugh and William Gallagher.

It was alleged that when the group reached the river, McHugh had lifted Mooney on to a wall and pushed him over – a drop of some 15ft – into the murky water. Gallagher was heard to say several times: 'God almighty, I won't do it!'

At the trial before Mr Justice Archibald, McHugh was convicted on the testimony of his erstwhile friends. Gallagher had been charged with murder as he had been identified as helping to carry Mooney down the passage towards the water, but he claimed that he did not know that McHugh planned to throw Mooney into the water. He was acquitted of the charge but censured by the judge for not preventing the murder from taking place. A motive was never clearly established, other than the quarrel that had taken place prior to the murder.

11

A POISON OF MICE AND MEN

❖ Elizabeth Pearson, 2 August 1875 ❖

Was it just a coincidence that the elderly man was taken ill days after arsenic-based poison appeared at his house? As the customer signed the poison register at the appropriately named Mr Corner's grocery shop, proprietor John Corner jokingly asked if she was buying it to poison someone. It was 2 March 1875 and it was the second such purchase of 'Battle's Vermin Powder' by 28-year-old Mrs Elizabeth Pearson in the last fortnight. Signing the register, she smiled at the weak joke: 'Oh no, it's a problem with mice.'

Elizabeth had been raised by her aunt and uncle at their home in Gainford since childhood. When her aunt died, she returned to the house to look after her uncle, John Watson, a 74-year-old retired shepherd. Watson lived in humble circumstances, relying on his small savings and rent from a lodger, George Smith.

By the spring of 1875, Mrs Pearson's husband had locked up their house and moved in with his wife at the old man's home. Soon gossip began to spread that Mrs Pearson's motives for moving in with her uncle were not simply charitable, and when the old man, who had long been suffering from a chest complaint, suddenly took a turn for the worse, Watson's estranged son Robert came to see his father. Although they had barely spoken in twenty years, he offered his father the chance to sell up and come and live with him in nearby Barnard Castle.

Hangman William Marwood. (Author's collection)

On the morning of Monday 15 March, lodger George Smith hurried to a neighbour and told her that the old man was 'none too well'. They returned to the house and found Elizabeth sitting beside his bed holding the man's wrists as he lay sweating, with his back arched as if in great agony. Within hours his condition had deteriorated and when Dr Homfrey, his regular doctor, arrived, John Watson had already passed away.

The neighbour sent a message to Watson's son but by the time he arrived in Gainsford at 9 p.m. that night, he was horrified to find that the house had been stripped of all furniture. The only item remaining in the house was a single bed – minus the mattress – on which the body of the old man lay.

Robert Watson rushed straight round to the Pearsons' house, where he found that all the furniture from his father's house already put to use. Mrs Pearson told him that the old man had wanted her to have the furniture, but such was the haste in which she had removed it, with the body of his father callously left on the bed frame, that Robert Watson contacted the police.

Detectives spoke to Dr Homfrey, who admitted that although he had been treating the old man for many years, his death had been quite sudden and was suspicious. Stomach contents were sent for analysis to a medical school in Leeds and produced interesting conclusions. Traces of Prussian-blue ferrocyanic acid, starch and strychnine were discovered – the ingredients of Battle's Vermin Powder. It was then a simple matter of speaking to local suppliers of the rodent killer to trace it to Mrs Pearson, and she was charged with murder.

Elizabeth Pearson was tried in front of Mr Justice Archibald at Durham Assizes on 8 July. The prosecution's claim that she had murdered her uncle in order to gain possession of his furniture was accepted by the jury, and she was convicted and sentenced to death. Pearson's defence tried to blame the lodger, who had since left the area, but there was never any doubt about the verdict. Asked if she had anything to say before sentence of death was passed, she told the court she was pregnant, but examinations while she was in the condemned cell proved the claim to be false.

She was hanged beside Gilligan and McHugh in the second and last triple execution at Durham Gaol. A crowd of over 300 gathered at the prison gates as hangman William Marwood went about his duties with ruthless efficiency.

12

THE HEAVY DRINKER

❖ *John Williams, 26 July 1876* ❖

Thirty-seven-year-old Welsh-born miner John Williams had moved with several members of his family to the north-east to find work, settling at Edmondsley, near Durham. On Friday 23 June 1876, Williams failed to go into work and spent the day in bed. Later that afternoon his son returned home from the day shift, bringing home his father's wage packet. When Williams rose he took half a sovereign from the wage packet and went out drinking. It had become a familiar habit, and it was drink that had prevented him going into work that day.

Mrs Williams, concerned at the amount of money he had taken, followed him into town and found him drinking in the Black Dene public house. Williams became enraged. Finishing his drink, he returned home and, after collecting a gun, went back to the pub. The landlord, seeing the clearly drunken Williams waving the firearm around, refused him entrance, while Mrs Williams, who had stayed in the pub chatting to friends, cowered in the kitchen. Williams waited outside but eventually gave up and went home, cursing his wife as he left.

Fearful for her safety, Mrs Williams decided to go to the house of her brothers, Joe and John Wales, telling them of her fears and her husband's threats. They offered to go to speak to Williams to try to calm the situation down. It was a fatal mistake. Williams was seemingly beyond reason and as the brothers approached the house he pointed the gun at them.

'You're not going to shoot, are you, Williams?' Joe shouted, and as Williams warned him to stand back, the gun discharged, hitting the younger brother, John Wales, in the arm. The ramrod, which was still in place, pierced the shoulder, punctured the lung and damaged the man's spine.

Realising what he had done, Williams stood in shock as his wife approached and disarmed him. Neighbours came out and as the younger brother was tended to, Williams was dragged to the police station. John Wales died from his injuries on the following morning.

Williams was tried before Mr Justice Lush on 5 July. There was no real defence offered, other than that he was drunk at the time and had not realised what he was doing. It was alleged that Williams was a heavy drinker and had spent six consecutive nights getting drunk in the same public house.

Passing sentence of death, the judge said he hoped it would be a warning to others, adding that this was another dreadful illustration of what drink could produce. Following the conviction, letters appeared in *The Times* censuring the pub landlord for allowing Williams to get drunk every night in the bar, and suggesting that drink should be available only at the weekend.

13

THE PREMONITION

❖ *Robert Vest, 30 July 1878* ❖

Although he had served his country well throughout the Crimean War, by the summer of 1878 32-year-old father of five Robert Vest had been out of work for a long period. It was therefore something of a relief to him when at the end of June he secured a position as a cook and steward aboard the *William Leckie*, a sailing barge moored at Sunderland Docks.

Under the command of Captain Fletcher, the boat was bound for South America with a cargo of coal and was due to depart on the afternoon of 26 June. On the morning of departure, Captain Fletcher travelled into Newcastle to collect some papers, but when he returned he found that the wind was insufficient to commence sailing and the voyage was delayed until the following morning.

Back on board, the Captain noticed that Vest appeared drunk and, after reprimanding him for bringing drink onto his ship, he told Vest he was being demoted to common seaman if he wanted to remain on the crew. Standing beside the captain was the pilot, John Wallace, who joked as Vest walked away, 'That's right, Captain, begin as you mean to end. Come aft, boys, and put him in irons!'

The loss of rank also meant a steep reduction in wages. Vest was already unhappy at being forced to leave his family while he earned a living, but least a steward's pay would have made the parting bearable. A lowly seaman's wage was a different matter and as Vest sat in his bunk he seethed.

As the crew whiled away the hours before departure, they were all served a quantity of grog, except Vest, although an apprentice later gave him a small amount of his ration. At 8.30 p.m. a fearful cry was heard coming from the deck. As members of the crew rushed to investigate, they found Vest dragging Pilot Wallace from the water closet. Wallace had been stabbed in the throat and abdomen with a large knife. The knife was left embedded in his stomach and after withdrawing it Wallace collapsed to the floor and died.

Before Vest was taken into custody, he told one of the crew, 'Something has been telling me for the last twenty-four years that I shall be hanged,' adding, 'I hope the poor man's soul has gone to heaven.'

At his trial before Lord Justice Baggallay on 12 July, Vest pleaded insanity. Evidence was heard that he was an avid reader of books on murder and his premonition of an ignominious death at the end of a hangman's rope was told to the jury. Just one month after he committed the brutal murder, Vest's fateful premonition came true.

14

A GRUESOME END TO A GRUESOME CRIME

❖ *William Brownless, 16 November 1880* ❖

William Brownless had a bad reputation. The stocky 22-year-old shoemaker was a foul-tempered heavy drinker and, although he held down regular employment in Butterknowle, he had a criminal record for robbery at a local drapery store.

Brownless had been courting publican's daughter Elizabeth Holmes, a 25-year-old farm hand who lived at nearby Evenwood, until one evening in the summer of 1880, when she told him she was ending their relationship. At 8 a.m. on the following morning, Wednesday 18 August, Brownless approached Elizabeth as she made her way to work. An hour later, a young man walking along the same path stumbled upon the bodies of the couple.

Each had severe throat wounds, but when they were taken to a nearby inn it was found that both were clinging to life. Elizabeth's throat had several cuts and her windpipe was severed completely; Brownless also had serious throat wounds and he had lost a large amount of blood. As a doctor was sent for, Brownless asked if Elizabeth was still alive. Such was his precarious state, they told Brownless that she was alive, even though it was clear she had since succumbed to her injuries. He then made a detailed statement.

Brownless said that he had waylaid her as she walked to work. When she repeated her assertion that she wanted nothing more to do with him and walked away to collect water from the well, he attacked her with a razor. He said the reason he had done it was that she had ended their relationship and refused his pleas to reconsider.

Brownless was sentenced to death by Mr Justice Field at Durham Crown Court on 29 October and, although he had suffered severe injuries to his neck, it was deemed safe for the execution to be carried out.

Executioner Marwood calculated a drop of almost 9ft and it was reported that the rope tore into his recently healed scar, spraying blood around the pit and almost severing the head. It was a gruesome end to a gruesome crime.

15

TO ESCAPE THE TORTURE OF GAOL

❖ *Thomas Fury, 16 May 1882* ❖

It was a murder that had long been filed as unsolved. On 19 February 1869, Maria Fitzsimmons, a 40-year-old prostitute who worked the docks at Sunderland, had been seen drinking in the company of a sailor. Early next morning her body was found in her room; she had ten stab wounds, nine of which had pierced her heart.

A sailor named Connor was arrested on the following day. He had been seen in the company of the woman shortly before her death and a tip-off naming him as the killer led to his arrest. As the investigation continued, detectives received a letter claiming that Connor was innocent and that the author was the real killer, who was now on his way to America. It was signed, 'A monster in human form'. With no real evidence against Connor, he was released and, despite a reward of £100 to catch the killer, the case remained unsolved.

Sunderland Docks, where Maria Fitzsimmons plied her trade. (Crime Picture Archive)

Ten years later, in the spring of 1879, Thomas Fury, aka Thomas Wright, aka Henry Charles Cort, a sailor, was arrested on a charge of burglary and attempted murder at Norwich. Soon after his arrest, he enquired whether the reward offered for information on the killing of Maria Fitzsimmons could still be claimed, as he said he could identify the killer. When he was told that it could not, he said no more about it. Tried for the attempted murder, he was sentenced to fifteen years in London's Pentonville Gaol.

Three years into the sentence, Fury asked to see a police inspector and confessed that he had murdered Maria Fitzsimmons. Fury said he had awoken after spending the night with her to find her attempting to strangle him with a cord. He knocked her down, pulled out his knife and stabbed her.

Taken back to Durham, the 31-year-old Irishman was tried before Mr Justice Watkins at the end of April. The evidence against him was based entirely on his own testimony, and it took less than an hour for the jury to find him guilty as charged. On the evening before he was hanged, Fury confided to a guard that he had confessed to clear his conscience and in order to escape the torture of gaol.

16

A BOTCHED EXECUTION

❖ *James Burton, 6 August 1883* ❖

When she discovered her new husband, James Burton, was not only a brutish bully but that he already had a wife about whom he had neglected to tell her, Elizabeth Burton told him that the marriage was over. The 18-year-old newly wed packed her bag and walked out of their marital home at Tunstall, near Sunderland, taking up the position as a live-in housemaid for a local solicitor. They had married in January 1883 and in just a matter of weeks it was all over.

Burton, the 33-year-old son of a police sergeant, made several vain attempts to see his wife, until finally on 8 May she agreed to his request to meet him. As they walked towards a railway bridge near Silksworth, witnesses heard a scream and saw a woman running along a railway embankment with a man in pursuit. A short time later an engine driver noticed something unusual lying next to the tracks. He stopped the engine and, adjacent to the line, he found the body of a woman partly concealed beneath large stones.

She was identified as Elizabeth Burton. A search soon located her husband in Sunderland, but, although he had bloodstains on his clothes, he denied that he had killed his wife. At his trial in July he maintained his innocence and said that his wife must have fallen from the bridge on to the railway line. He was convicted on circumstantial evidence and sentenced to death by Mr Justice Watkins in July. Awaiting execution, he confessed that he had killed his wife during a quarrel by battering her about the head with a stone after she had struck him with an umbrella.

His execution was to be the last carried out by celebrated Victorian hangman William Marwood. For the last decade, Marwood, now an ailing and sick man, had refined the art of execution, working out a method of calculating a specific drop based on the weight of the prisoner. In what was known as the 'long drop' method, Marwood favoured giving the condemned prisoners drops of anything between 5 and 10ft, producing instant death by dislocation of the spinal column.

Burton had borne up well in the condemned cell and rose at 7 a.m., when the chaplain joined him. On the stroke of 8, Marwood pinioned the condemned man's arms in the cell, and although Burton was very pale, he walked to the drop with a firm step. At 3 minutes past 8, with the prisoner positioned on the trapdoor, and satisfied that all was ready, Marwood pulled the lever. Witnesses were aghast to see the rope swing violently from side to side and it was clear that something was amiss.

Looking into the pit, Marwood could see that the slack of the rope had caught under the prisoner's elbow and had prevented the fall from breaking his neck. With the aid of a warder, Burton was hoisted out of the pit and the rope readjusted. Twice, the condemned man was heard to cry, 'O Lord have mercy on my poor soul,' before the hangman and warder pushed the condemned man back into the pit. Although the rope once more swung vigorously from side to side for several minutes, this time death was deemed to be instant.

Making a report after the execution, Marwood said that he had hurried the proceedings as he sensed that the prisoner was about to faint. He recommended that, to prevent a repetition, planks should be placed across the drop to allow warders to support the condemned man should he faint and, most significantly, that the rope should be coiled up above the height of the noose so that there would be no risk of fouling when the trapdoor opened. These small but significant recommendations became his final legacy: they were adopted throughout the country and remained in place until abolition. Within weeks of the botched execution, William Marwood was himself dead.

How the Illustrated Police News *recorded the botched execution of James Burton*. (Crime Picture Archive)

17

THE STRIKEBREAKER

❖ *Peter Bray, 24 November 1883* ❖

On the morning of Sunday 2 April 1882, the body of a man was found on a footpath at Priors Path. He had been stabbed in the throat with a large nail, similar to those used in the adjacent fence. The victim was identified as Thomas Pyle, a platelayer at Ushaw Moor Colliery, and police soon found a likely motive when it was known that threats had recently been made against Pyle. Detectives learned that earlier that year there had been a strike at the colliery and that when Pyle had refused to join in the walk-out, he was labelled a blackleg and became the object of abuse and threats.

Police interviewed scores of workers at the colliery but, while many agreed that they had made verbal threats against the dead man, there was no evidence linking anyone to the crime. A reward of £200 also failed to bring any leads and gradually the investigation wound down.

One man whom police had interviewed several times during the investigation was 32-year-old Peter Bray, a miner and former soldier in the Hartlepool militia. With a long history of criminal convictions, he had served a number of prison terms, including a seven-year sentence for robbery with violence at Crossgate Peth, Durham, and had once received twenty-five lashes of the cat. A tip-off from a former cell-mate led police to arrest Bray as he walked out of Durham Gaol after serving another sentence.

He stood trial before Mr Justice Day on 2 November. The prosecution alleged that the motive was simply that Pyle had been a strikebreaker, who had enraged Bray to the extent that he had killed him. Several witnesses had since come forward stating that they had seen Pyle in a drunken heap collapsed close to where he was found murdered. Bray was among a crowd of men who passed, and when he learned who the drunk was he declared that he would 'away back and kill the bastard'. His defence claimed that the main prosecution witnesses were all lying and that the evidence against him had been fabricated in order to claim the £200 reward. Following conviction, however, he wrote out a full confession.

Bray was hanged by Bartholomew Binns of Dewsbury, who had taken over from Marwood as the chief executioner. It was Binns's only visit to Durham in his short reign as the 'number one', which was quickly terminated following a catalogue of botched executions across the country. Fortunately for Bray, his execution was one of the few that went smoothly. Bray twice made a request to speak to reporters as he stood on the trapdoor, but permission was refused. Seconds later the drop fell and it was reported that in this case death was instant.

18

DEATH ON DUTY

❖ *Joseph Lowson, 28 May 1884* ❖

Saturday 23 February 1884 had turned into a rainy and cold evening, not the kind of night to be out on the streets. Earlier that afternoon, three young miners, James Hodgson, Joseph Lowson and William Siddle, had attended a pigeon-shooting handicap at the Diamond Inn, Butterknowle and, unwilling to venture home in the bad weather, had spent the evening drinking in the bar.

At ten o'clock, when the landlord called last orders, they reluctantly drank up and, as they made their way from the pub, they spotted police Sergeant William Smith standing across the road watching them. William Siddle had a history of run-ins with Sergeant Smith in previous years, culminating in his committing an assault on the officer, which led to a court appearance and hefty fine.

After walking just a short distance, the three men, all the worse for drink, turned back and began antagonising Smith. Sensing that he could make the situation worse by engaging in any sort of confrontation, the sergeant walked off. As other customers filed out of the pub, the three men were seen to follow in the direction Smith had taken.

A short time later, the sergeant was found beaten to death in a field. As a doctor tended vainly to the stricken policeman, witnesses noticed that the three men were watching from across the street before they turned and disappeared into the night.

Once the officer had been certified dead, a murder investigation began and police started to round up men who matched the description of the three seen watching as Smith lay dying. The three miners were arrested on suspicion and, when traces of blood were found on the shirt of one of them, they were all charged with murder.

The three stood trial together before Mr Justice Hawkins at Durham Assizes on 3 May. The evidence was mainly circumstantial: no one had witnessed the attack but the bloodstains from Lowson's shirt and a missing button, identical to one found next to the body of the policeman, were enough to convince the jury. Hodgson was acquitted of all charges, while the other two were convicted of murder and sentenced to death, despite claims that police had fabricated evidence against them.

Siddle strongly protested his innocence from the death cell and wrote a letter to the Home Secretary, which was enough for the executions to be postponed for one week while the evidence was reviewed. They were rescheduled for Wednesday 28 May. Lowson told his brother that it was Hodgson who should be awaiting the hangman with him, not Siddle, and with just days before the scheduled execution, a reprieve was announced in the case of Siddle.

Joseph Lowson, who weighed over 16 stone, was the first man hanged at Durham Gaol by the new executioner, James Berry. He showed no fear at the prospect of being hanged, and joked with a warder who had guarded him in the death cell that he would see him again soon. As the white cap was placed over his head, he made a final statement admitting his guilt but claiming that Hodgson had struck the first blow.

19

THE GATESHEAD RIPPER

❖ *William Waddell, 18 December 1888* ❖

Was it the work of Jack the Ripper? Police at Gateshead investigating the brutal murder and mutilation of Jane Beetmore on Birtley Fell, near Gateshead, suspected it might be, and wasted no time in calling for the assistance of Scotland Yard. It was the autumn of 1888 and newspapers up and down the country were full of the horrific crime wave that had left a trail of mutilated corpses across the Whitechapel district of London.

The body had been found in a ditch close to a wagon track. She had been stabbed below the ear; the knife had cut the throat and almost severed the spinal cord. There was another wound to the head, but what suggested that it might be the work of the 'Ripper' was the horrific knife wounds to the chest and abdomen.

Inspector Roots and Dr Phillips left London on the following morning, while detectives in Durham began their investigations. They soon had a likely suspect in 22-year-old ironworker William Waddell, who had been courting Miss Beetmore for several months and who now seemed to be missing from the area.

It was learned that Jane had been recently discharged from a local hospital and had set out on the evening of Saturday 22 September to buy some sweets to take with her medicine. When she had failed to return home, a search was organised and her body discovered on the following morning. Investigations into the movements of Waddell found that he had returned to his lodgings on Saturday afternoon the worse for drink and had gone out again in the early evening. They also learned from friends of the dead girl that she had told Waddell recently that she wished to end their relationship and that he had been pestering her for another chance.

It was soon ascertained that the wounds on the murdered girl were unlikely to be the work of the Whitechapel killer and, satisfied that the answer to their mystery was closer to home, the Scotland Yard men left the region to pursue their own ongoing investigations in London.

Waddell was arrested on Monday 1 October at Yetholm in Roxburghshire, Scotland. His movements had been charted through Berwick, where he purchased a second-hand suit, part-exchanging his own in the process. This suit was taken away for investigation, where it was tested for bloodstains.

Waddell was convicted before Mr Justice Baron Pollack on 29 October. His defence was twofold: that he was drunk at the time of the crime, which he had no knowledge of committing, and also that he was insane at the time.

His execution was scheduled for Tuesday 18 December 1888, and hangman Berry arrived in the city on the Monday afternoon. After testing the apparatus, Berry left the prison for a teatime stroll and recorded going into a hotel, where they where discussing the murder. Asked by a stranger what he thought of the crime, Berry said it was a brutal murder. The man said that he did not believe that Waddell should be hanged and that he would like to hang Berry himself!

Berry, who would on occasion often surprise an inquisitive stranger by presenting his business card, thus calmly revealing his identity, declined to do so on this occasion and returned quickly to the gaol.

On the morning of the execution, he found Waddell waiting as he entered the cell, seemingly indifferent to his fate. 'Hurry up and I will not give you a moment longer to suffer,' Berry said as he strapped his wrists. Waddell made no sound but walked firmly to the gallows, where moments later Jane Beetmore was avenged.

20

THE WEDDING DAY MURDER

❖ *John Johnson, 22 December 1891* ❖

For John Johnson, the news was just about the worst he could have imagined. For the best part of twenty years he had been courting his former landlady, 52-year-old Margaret Addison, at Hetton-le-Hole until his intemperate habits had caused her to end their relationship. Not only had he lost the woman he loved; the 49-year-old agricultural labourer then found himself homeless.

Since the break-up, Mrs Addison had begun courting a local coal miner, Andrew Simpson, and, within a short time, made plans to get married. Johnson took this news badly and a few days later acquired a revolver.

On Saturday 31 October 1891, Mrs Addison put on her wedding clothes and in the company of her bridesmaids and relatives made her way from her home at Four Lane Ends, down Station Road in the direction of the church. As she passed a public house close to the station, Johnson watched from a window. He put down his empty glass, walked outside and approached Margaret. He spoke to her but she seemed to ignore him, whereupon he pulled out the gun and fired two shots into her head, killing her instantly. He then walked to the local police station, where he surrendered and made a full confession.

He chose to plead guilty at his trial before Mr Justice Wills at Durham Crown Court, stating that he understood the course he was taking and appreciated the consequences. In passing sentence, the judge commented: 'I am not surprised at the course you have taken, although it is a course unprecedented in my experience.'

It was a simple, sad story, actuated by jealousy. Johnson was determined that the woman who would not marry him would not marry anyone else instead.

21

THE LAST-MINUTE CONFESSION

❖ *Charles Smith, 22 March 1898* ❖

Charles Smith put down his trowel and decided to clock off for the day. It was Monday 27 December 1897 and the Aberdeen-born plasterer left the building site at Jesmond, heading straight to a local public house. In the company of workmate George Kirkpatrick, he stayed until afternoon closing time, whereupon they went back to Smith's rented apartment in a run-down tenement block at Pipewellgate, Gateshead.

Smith changed out of his work clothes and drank a glass of whisky. He then picked up his accordion and, together with Kirkpatrick, went out to meet up with another workmate, Paddy Welsh. They embarked on a pub crawl until Kirkpatrick called it a day at 6 p.m. At seven o'clock, Smith and Welsh were roaring drunk. Smith decided to go home, where he found that his wife, Mary Ann, had visitors.

By 11.30 p.m. Smith and his wife were alone, but a couple of hours later their son woke to find his parents fighting downstairs. Mary Ann was subsequently found dead, with severe head injuries caused by a broom handle. Smith was arrested but denied that he had committed the murder, insisting that he had found his wife in this state. Bloodstains on his clothes suggested otherwise and he was taken into custody.

Smith maintained his innocence throughout his detention and at his trial at Durham on 3 March 1898. Faced with a strong case from the prosecution, the defence focused on the question of intention to kill, hoping that if the defendant was convicted it would be on a lesser charge of manslaughter. They jury took less than an hour to find him guilty as charged and Smith heard the verdict white-faced. 'I never did anything,' he cried as sentence of death was passed, and his cries were still audible as he was ushered from the dock.

Petitions for mercy were gathered in his native Aberdeen but they failed to sway the Home Secretary; the execution was to go ahead as scheduled. Smith broke down completely when he heard there was to be no reprieve and spent his last hours on earth in a daze. On the morning of his execution he kept up the pretence that he was innocent until moments before the hangman entered the cell. Under pressure from the priest to repent his sins, Smith finally made a last-minute confession.

'I am very sorry I did it,' he said as the condemned cell door opened and James Billington and his son Thomas entered. Charles Smith was the first person to be hanged in the new, purpose-built, brick-walled execution chamber, walking the few short steps to his doom with his conscience clear.

22

MURDER ON THE BEACH

❖ *John Bowes, 12 December 1900* ❖

Isabella Bowes had led a hard life. She had an unemployed husband, who treated her badly, abused and beat both her and her 21-year-old daughter, and refused to contribute to the upkeep of his family. The 50-year-old wife and mother was, however, industrious and was able to provide something for the family by picking coal off the beach at Seaham Harbour to put food on the table. On a good day she would earn four or five shillings, but it was sporadic and unreliable and often a whole day's work would yield barely a shilling or two.

But it could have been different. She was married to a skilled craftsman: her husband, 50-year-old John Bowes, was a bricklayer by trade, although he now preferred to idle his life away drinking and quarrelling with his wife. He seemed to have believed that his wife was cheating on him, although there is no evidence of any impropriety on her part, when on 21 August 1900, during a particularly violent drunken quarrel, he struck her and tore up her daughter's clothes.

CERTIFICATE OF SURGEON.

31 *Vic. Cap.* 24.

I, Philip Francis Gilbert the Surgeon of Her Majesty's Prison of Durham hereby certify that I this day examined the Body of John Bowes, on whom Judgment of Death was this day executed in the said Prison; and that on that Examination I found that the said John Bowes was dead.

Dated this 12th *day of* December, 1900

(Signature), P. F. Gilbert

Official notice of the execution of John Bowes. (Crime Picture Archive)

Isabella had tried her best to put up with his unreasonable behaviour but now she had reached the end of her tether. When he threatened to kill the pair of them, she left, taking her daughter with her, and went to stay with her uncle. In a rage, Bowes swore that he would get even with them.

On 8 September, Bowes saw his wife on the beach at Seaham Harbour. He strode towards her, where, after a brief argument, he picked up a heavy piece of wood and lashed out. As Isabella fell to the ground, Bowes repeatedly struck her about the head until she lapsed into unconsciousness. Realising what he had done, Bowes knelt down and cradled his wife's head in his arms as witnesses to the horrific attack hurried to fetch the police. Isabella was taken to hospital, but never recovered consciousness and died a few hours later.

At his trial before Mr Justice Grantham in November, Bowes readily admitted his guilt and seemed genuinely remorseful for the crime.

23

THE RESULT OF A PETTY THEFT

John Thompson, 10 December 1901

Thirty-eight-year-old John George Thompson was a popular and well-liked worker who earned a good wage as an engine fitter at Gateshead. However, his world seemed to fall apart when, in July 1901, he stole a number of metal files from work and ended up in court, charged with theft. The resulting fine and the shame he felt at the conviction caused him to leave his job and break up with his sweetheart.

Maggie Ann Lieutand was already married to someone else when she met Thompson early in 1901. The marriage was not a happy one and she left to move in with Thompson, but this relationship also quickly deteriorated and they had split up by the time Thompson's case came to court.

Thompson roamed the north-east for several weeks before returning to Gateshead in September, whereupon he took to making repeated desperate efforts to persuade Maggie to return to him. His pleas fell upon deaf ears.

On 16 September Thompson bought a six-chambered revolver and fifty cartridges. On the following day he went to seek out Maggie Ann Lieutand. He found her in the company of her landlady, a Mrs Dawson. He watched as they returned to her lodgings, and as they reached the door he approached. Thompson grabbed Maggie's arm and pleaded

Brothers William and Thomas Billington hanged John Thompson at Durham three days before the death of their father, James, who had originally been engaged to carry out the execution. (Author's collection)

with her to return to him. She struggled from his grasp and repeated that she wanted nothing more to do with him. Mrs Dawson also told him to stay away and stop bothering Maggie. The women hurried on and entered the house, trying to close the door behind them. Thompson forced his way in, withdrawing his gun as he did so. A shot rang out and Maggie was struck in the shoulder.

It was clear that Thompson intended to commit murder and Mrs Dawson shouted for Maggie to run. Maggie rushed across the street with Thompson in pursuit. As she entered a friend's house, Thompson forced his foot into the doorway. Maggie could not close the door, but neither could Thompson force it open. After a brief struggle, he managed to widen the gap sufficiently to get the gun through and, aiming in her direction, fired twice more. The first bullet struck Maggie in the arm; the second and ultimately fatal shot struck her in the head. Stung by remorse, Thompson began to cradle Maggie in his arms, where she was heard to say, 'Don't, Jack, I love you!' Thompson gave himself up when the police arrived and, as he handed over the gun, readily admitted responsibility for the shooting.

At his trial before Mr Justice Grantham at Durham Assizes on 22 November, Thompson's defence was one of temporary insanity, made at the request of his legal advisers in an attempt to reduce the charge to one of manslaughter and avoid the gallows. The plea having failed, John George Thompson, whose life turned upside down as a result of a petty theft, was duly convicted of murder.

24

AS RED AS GUILTY BLOOD

❖ Thomas Nicholson, 16 December 1902 ❖

Seven-year-old Mary Ina Stewart disappeared after a visit to her aunt and uncle's home at Gosforth Terrace, Newcastle. She had spent the afternoon of Saturday 16 August 1902 with her relatives when, at 7.30 p.m., she set off for the short trip home. Mary was grown up for her age and, her home being just a ten-minute walk along a hilly footpath past Bill Quay quarry, it was felt that it was safe enough for her to make the journey alone.

When Mary failed to return home that night, the police were notified and a search organised, but it was to be over thirty-six hours later, on the Monday morning, before her body was discovered. Friends searching the quarry grounds 150 yards from the footpath discovered the body of Mary Stewart. She had been stabbed, raped and finally strangled to death.

As detectives retraced Mary's footsteps on the Saturday night, they learned that a man had been seen on the footpath at the time she disappeared; and, crucially, another witness

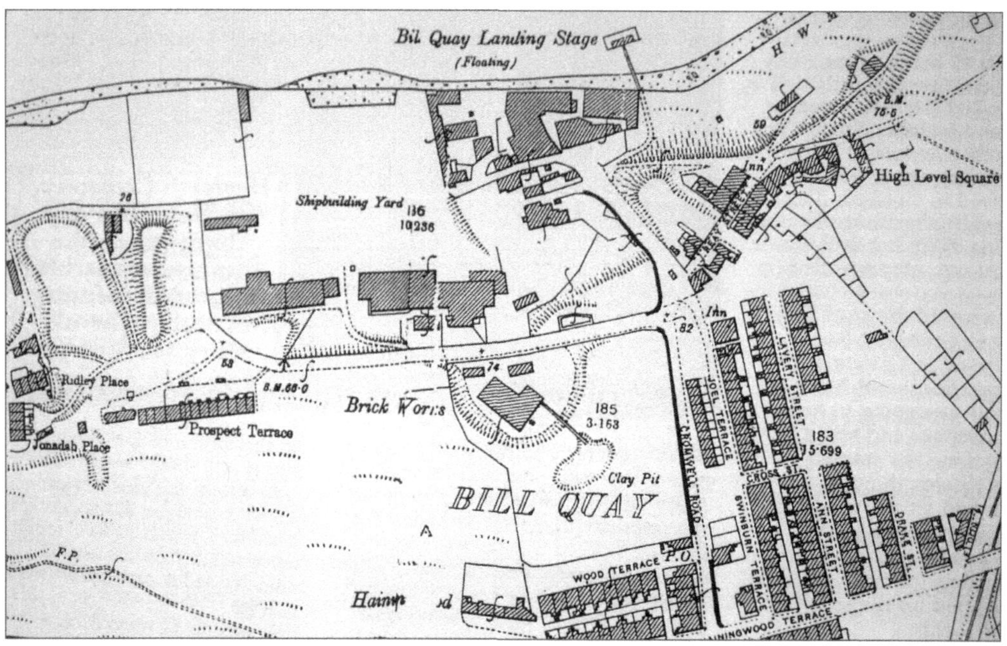

Map showing Bill Quay quarry at the turn of the century. (Crime Picture Archive)

came forward to say that he had seen a man holding hands with a young girl on the path at around 8 p.m.

One name that cropped up early in the investigation was that of Thomas Nicholson, a 24-year-old labourer. His description matched that of the man seen on the footpath on Saturday night, he was known to have been in the area around the Bill Quay pathway at around eight o'clock on the night Mary was last seen, and when detectives called to his house they found other evidence linking him to the crime. The pair of trousers he had been wearing on the Saturday evening bore traces of blood and there were also bloodstains on Nicholson's shirt and coat. Most crucially, they also found a bloodstained pocket knife, the blade of which was the same type as the one that had been used to stab the young girl.

John Billington assisted his brother at three executions at Durham, and carried out one as chief executioner. (Author's collection)

Although Nicholson was not clearly identified as the man seen with Mary on the footpath, he had been seen in the area. When asked to account for his movements after six o'clock on 16 August, he claimed he had been drinking in the Mason's Arms at the time Mary went missing and had only left at closing time. When his alibi was checked, it was found that, although witnesses identified him as having been in the pub, several customers claimed they had seen Nicholson, the worse for drink, leave the pub a little after 6.30 p.m. It was also found that he had pawned a suit on the Monday following the murder, and when this was reclaimed it was found to have traces of blood.

Although the evidence against him was in the main circumstantial, it was nevertheless enough for detectives to charge him with wilful murder. In due course Nicholson found himself standing before Mr Justice Channell at Durham Assizes on 24 November. Prosecution counsel J.E. Joel outlined the evidence step by step and highlighted that Nicholson had lied when he said he was in the public house at the time Mary Stewart went missing. Why, he asked, should he make this claim unless it was to hide something?

Asked to account for the bloodstains on the suit of clothes retrieved from the pawnshop and which he was alleged to have been wearing on the night Mary Stewart was killed, Nicholson repeated his claims of innocence, claiming simply that 'Innocent blood is as red as guilty blood.'

Circumstantial evidence it may have been, but it was enough to convince the jury of Nicholson's guilt. He made no reply when sentence of death was passed, merely hanging his head as the black cap was draped upon the judge's wig.

25

PAYMENT WITH A BULLET

❖ *Samuel Thomas Walton, 16 December 1902* ❖

The marriage had not been a happy one from the start and, after nine years fraught with fights and feuds, matters finally came to a head. Late on the night of 23 August 1902, Samuel Walton, a 32-year-old Spennymoor-born miner, finally lost patience with his wife Isabella and turned both her and their young child out on to the street. She went to stay at her mother's house, from where on the following day she decided to make steps to end the troubled marriage officially.

Taking legal advice, she chose to take out a separation order on the grounds of her husband's persistent cruelty, and on 4 September she was granted custody of her child and a maintenance order of 10s a week against her husband, the first payment to be made in seven days. On hearing this news, Walton became enraged.

On 9 September, he sold all his furniture and left his home at Middlestone Moor. On the following day, he purchased a Bulldog revolver and a box of fifty cartridges from a pawnshop at Tudhoe Grange, and that night, as he sat drinking with friends at the Mason's Arms, he showed them the gun and said, 'I have my first ten shillings to pay tomorrow and I will likely pay it with this.' They were chilling words.

The next day, he turned up at his mother-in-law's house on Albion Street. Isabella's mother, Mrs Isabella Young, answered the door and Walton told her he had come to pay the first ten shillings. 'I want a receipt for this,' he demanded and, as Mrs Young made to go upstairs to fetch a pen and paper, he drew out his gun and shot her through the temple. She died instantly.

Bursting into the house, Walton sought out his wife and shot her three times in the head. Then, taking his young daughter Esther in his arms, he placed the gun against her head and pulled the trigger. Although mortally wounded, Isabella Walton managed to escape from the house, where she told a neighbour, 'My mother is dead, my baby is dead and I am dying.'

Cradling the murdered child in his arms, Walton went upstairs, lay down on the bed and cut his own throat. Police were soon at the scene and Walton was rushed to Auckland Hospital, were his wounds were found to be mainly superficial. A week later, with Walton now transferred to Durham Gaol, Isabella Walton died from her injuries. When Walton stood trial before Mr Justice Channell, it was on the charge of triple murder.

His defence offered a plea of manslaughter, stating that Walton was distraught at the break-up of his marriage. The prosecution pointed out that Walton had hardly been distraught when he had ejected his wife from their home and that the reason for the murder was more likely anger at the demands for money imposed by the separation order. There was clear premeditation in purchasing the gun from the pawnshop and showing it to friends on the night before the murders, when he had boasted that he would use it to make the first payment.

26

IMMORAL EARNINGS

❖ *James Duffy, 8 December 1903* ❖

Twenty-five-year-old Eleanor 'Nellie' Newman made her living as a prostitute and, for the last twelve months, James Duffy, a 46-year-old widowed labourer, had lived off her immoral earnings. Since the summer of 1902 they had shared a house at Windsor Terrace, Grangetown, but it was a volatile relationship. In November of that year, Duffy received a one-month prison sentence, with hard labour, for assaulting her, although on his release she was happy to take him back.

Not only was 6ft, muscularly built Duffy a violent man, but he was also lazy and seemed not to care if Nellie slept with other men for money; as long as he did not have to work, he could put up with it. Money was often short and Duffy, despite his reluctance to find work, blamed Nellie.

In early September 1903, following an argument, Nellie walked out of their house in Back North Durham Street, Sunderland, declaring she 'could no longer live with a pig like him'. Duffy persuaded her to return to the house but, on the morning of Sunday 6 September, he walked to the local police station and confessed to murder: 'I have come to give myself up, I can't stand it any longer.'

Police went to the house and found Nellie Newman lying across a bed. She had been strangled. Duffy admitted grabbing her by the throat but said that he did not mean to kill her, adding that she was dead before he realised what he was doing.

At his trial before Mr Justice Grantham at Durham Assizes, Duffy offered a weak defence of murder in the course of self-defence, following a quarrel over money. It was to no avail.

27

MORE THAN ANYTHING ELSE IN THE WORLD

❖ *George Breeze, 2 August 1904* ❖

Coal miner and semi-professional footballer George Breeze broke the golden rule of friendship when he fell in love with his best friend's wife. Twenty-one-year-old Breeze had taken lodging with the Chisholms in June 1904 following a dispute with his father. Both Chisholm and Breeze were popular players for Seaham White Star, and Breeze in particular, with his fine physique and handsome looks, soon made an impression on Margaret Jane Chisholm.

Chisholm's offer to George to share his home was indeed a kind gesture, as home on Back Church Street, Dawden, was nothing more than one room which housed Chisholm, his wife, their 2-year-old daughter and the new lodger. Within weeks, Breeze had fallen in love with his new landlady. In turn, Margaret was unhappy in her relationship with her husband and began to reciprocate the feeling. Chisholm soon began to suspect that something was going on. As he and Breeze worked different shifts, he often had to go to work leaving his wife in bed and his friend asleep on the adjacent sofa.

On Wednesday 6 July, Margaret prepared her husband's breakfast, and once he had left for work she woke Breeze and broke down in tears. She told him she had confessed to her husband about her feelings for Breeze and he had told her she had to make a choice before he returned home. She told him she wished that she was dead. Breeze was equally distraught. He had fallen madly in love and knew that whatever choice she made would cost him either his home and friendship, or the woman he loved. He had already had to suffer the agonies of sharing the room with Margaret and her husband as they lay in bed together, feet away from where he slept.

He asked Margaret if she really wanted to die. She told him she no longer cared if she lived or died, but it probably did not occur to her that he would have the heart to do it. Breeze put his hands tightly around her throat and squeezed. Leaving Margaret's young child alone in the house, he closed the door and walked to the nearby police station. He made no plans to escape. On the table beside the body he left a written confession. As police went to the house to follow up Breeze's admission, he wrote out a detailed statement at the station, describing the depth of his feelings for the woman he had just killed.

Breeze appeared before Mr Justice Grantham at Durham Assizes just ten days later. In his eagerness to pay the ultimate price for his crime, he fully cooperated in the report confirming that he was fit to stand trial, insisting on pleading guilty and refusing to be defended by counsel.

Asked if he had anything to say before sentence of death was passed, Breeze told the court that he loved Margaret more than anything else in the world, that he was not sorry for what he had done and was now quite ready to die. He thanked the judge following the passing of the death sentence, adding that he hoped there would be no reprieve. His wish was granted three weeks later.

28

I KILLED HER . . . I WILL SWING FOR HER

❖ *Robert William Lawman, 24 March 1908* ❖

Even the normally staid judge had tears in his eyes as he carried out his sombre duties. As the clerk of the court draped the small square of black cloth upon his wig, the silence in the court was heavy with emotion. Steeling himself, Mr Justice Channell pronounced sentence of death upon Robert Lawman.

Lawman, a 32-year-old Cumberland miner, had been separated from his wife and sons for some four years, and since then he had lived with barmaid and part-time prostitute Amelia Wood, while he found work in the mines around Gateshead.

On Thursday 30 January 1908, Amelia turned up at a lodging house in Hyde Park Street, Gateshead, asking for a room. Later that night, Lawman joined her and at noon the next day he gave the landlady, Mrs Elizabeth Senior, money for some beer and whisky, which she had purchased for them.

Elizabeth returned to the kitchen to cook the breakfast Amelia had ordered, when she heard a low moan from the barmaid's room. Thinking she may be ill, Elizabeth called out and tried the door. Finding it locked and receiving no answer, she returned to the kitchen, only to be stopped in her tracks by a blood-curdling scream.

Again she called out and tried the door, but on this occasion wasted no time and ran out into the street, returning with two policemen. They forced their way into the room to discover Lawman leaning over Amelia, who had a horrific throat wound. Lawman was also suffering from a self-inflicted neck wound. Both were rushed to hospital, but it was too late for Amelia Wood, who died in the ambulance. Taken in for questioning, Lawman immediately confessed: 'I loved her. I killed her. I will swing for her.'

At his trial, the story of their relationship was revealed. Lawman was heartbroken when he discovered that she was working as a prostitute, and when she realised that he had learned her secret she told him that they should part. Feeling that he could not live without her, he vowed then he would kill her and then himself. Only prompt medical attention had prevented him carrying out that side of the plan.

'I thank you, my Lord,' he said, addressing the judge as the sentence of death was passed over him. Three weeks later, the hangman's rope helped him achieve what the razor had failed to do.

29

YOU MIGHT BREAK MY NECK . . .

Joseph William Noble, 24 March 1908

The staff at Windy Nook Co-operative Society store, Gateshead, decided it was time for action. There had been a number of burglaries at the Windy Nook branch and four committee members – John Patterson, Christopher Carr, George Ather and Joseph Cowell – decided to mount an all-night vigil at the shop. The first stakeouts came to nothing, but on the night of 31 October 1907 they again took up their positions, the lamps were dimmed and they waited.

This time their luck was in. At just after 4 in the morning, they heard a noise, a door handle turned and a dark figure entered the room. Cowell turned up the lamp, revealing a masked man dressed in dark clothes, carrying a miner's lamp. The four leaped on him and a violent struggle ensued. The intruder fought hard as they attacked him with a stool and a hammer. Managing to reach into his jacket pocket he pulled out a gun. A shot rang out and Patterson, struck in the head, fell down dead. Another bullet caught Cowell in the top of the leg and, as he too fell to the ground, the defenders backed away while the burglar made his escape.

George Ather's wife, who lived across from the store, heard the shots and, picking up an axe, went over to investigate. Dressed just in her nightdress, she saw the intruder as he slipped out of a side window at the store and she bravely gave chase, wielding the axe, only for him to disappear into the night.

A number of clues had been left behind at the shop, including a skeleton key and several clear footprints. Police began their hunt for the burglar, who, they reasoned, would have sustained noticeable injuries during the disturbance. This led them to interview Joseph Noble, a 48-year-old blacksmith on the LNER railway. Covered in bruises, he claimed they were as a result of a fall at work, but his footprints matched those found at the scene and a search of his home turned up jemmies and other burglar's tools. Placed under arrest, he was found to have injuries to the head and bruises on his legs, which would tie in with a beating from a hammer. A search of his house found a box of cartridges of the same type as those that had been fired at the store, plus a quantity of goods that had been reported as stolen from the Co-op store in recent weeks.

At his two-day trial in March, Noble stated that he was not in Windy Nook on the night of the murder. He claimed that he kept and used the miner's lantern found at his home when feeding his ferrets. Although he denied owning a gun, he admitted that he often repaired guns for pitmen who lived nearby. He explained that the bruising on his leg was caused at his work as a blacksmith.

Windy Nook killer Joseph Noble. (T.J. Leech archive)

Circumstantial evidence it may all have been, but it was enough for the jury to find him guilty of murder after a deliberation of just forty-five minutes. Asked by Mr Justice Channell if he had anything to say before being sentenced, Noble replied, 'You might break my neck but I don't think you will break my heart.'

He was hanged alongside another Gateshead murderer, cutthroat killer Robert Lawman, by Henry Pierrepoint and his brother Tom. Noble and Lawman weighed the same, 178lb, and the hangman noted that they were among the heaviest men he had ever hanged. Lawman received a drop of 6ft; Noble's neck was broken with a drop of 6ft 10in.

30

THE RIGHT TO AN APPEAL

❖ *Matthew James Dodds, 5 August 1908* ❖

It was felt from the outset that there was more behind the death of 50-year-old Mary Jane Dodds in February 1908 than at first appeared. It was reported as an accident, the coroner had recorded an open verdict and her funeral had gone ahead as planned. The initial suspicions were, however, soon to be justified. As more information came into their possession, police ordered an exhumation. A second post-mortem was to lead to a man standing trial for his life and a historic first sitting of the Court of Criminal Appeal.

Owning her own home and several other properties in the village of Hamsterley, Mary Jane Dodds was a wealthy woman. In February 1907, after two years of marriage, she made a will leaving all her worldly goods to husband Matthew Dodds. Theirs was not a happy marriage, however, and neighbours would often hear them arguing and shouting at each other.

Six months later, Mary drew up a new will, this time leaving her husband hardly anything. But things seemed to turn around and, by January 1908, Dodds had persuaded her to draw up yet another will. As in the first, she once more left everything to her husband.

On 20 February, Dodds hurried from the house and called on a neighbour, saying that there had been a terrible accident and his wife lay dead in the fireplace. He claimed that he had returned home from spending the afternoon at his father's joinery shop and found her dead. His version of events was believed. Following an inquest, the body was released for burial and Dodds laid his wife to rest in the local churchyard.

Soon the rumours and gossip began. One neighbour stated that she had heard raised voices from the Dodds's house shortly before he claimed to have returned home. Police made their own enquiries and, learning about the series of wills, they began to have their suspicions. Just seventeen days after she had been interred, a crowd assembled in the churchyard as the body of Mary Jane Dodds was exhumed. This time, the pathologist concluded that death was due to strangulation.

Tried before Mr Justice Grantham on 1 July, Dodds maintained that he had come home to find his wife lying dead in the grate. It was stated that she had died at around 2.30 p.m. on Thursday 20 February and evidence suggested that Dodds was present at the time. Although Dodds asserted that he was at work at this time, there was no evidence to support his claims and he was duly convicted and sentenced to death.

In the period between the murder and his conviction, a new ruling had been passed that gave Dodds the chance to argue his case for one last time. Dodds was the first convicted murderer to be granted an appeal. Appearing before a panel that consisted of the Lord Chief Justice, Mr Justice Darling and Mr Justice Walton on 17 July, under the new Criminal Appeal Act, Dodds's defence argued that the verdict should be revoked on account of a flaw in the judge's summing-up. They claimed that evidence had not been called at the trial to support Dodds's claims he had been away from the house at the time of the murder, which had been crucial to his defence.

Dismissing the appeal, the panel found that there was nothing wrong in the summing-up by Mr Justice Grantham, and that the evidence presented in court had been strong enough for the jury to return the guilty verdict.

31

MURDER AT WEST STANLEY

❖ Jeremiah O'Connor, 23 February 1909 ❖

For three years, 52-year-old coal miner Jeremiah O'Connor lodged at the home of Thomas Donnelly and his family at Pool Street, West Stanley. Irish-born O'Connor was an honest, hard-working tenant whose only vice seemed to be a fondness for drink. On Saturday 12 December 1908, O'Connor celebrated the weekend by visiting his local pub. He drank continuously throughout the weekend, so much so that he was unable to go into work on the Monday morning.

Having spent the day in bed recovering, he was up and about by the evening and at around 8.45 p.m., 10-year-old Mary Donnelly, the landlord's daughter, was seen with O'Connor, walking down a lane at Gibside, some 4 miles from her home. When both she and O'Connor failed to return home that night, police were informed and started their search the next morning.

The search continued throughout the week without success and it was not until the following Saturday that O'Connor was picked up. He had been living rough in woods near Tonfield and claimed to have no information about the disappearance of Mary. He collapsed when placed under arrest, and with feelings running high it was decided to take him to Consett to avoid the angry lynch mob that had gathered as investigations continued.

Less than twenty-four hours later, police made the gruesome discovery when a body was found hidden beneath bushes on a quiet lane close to her home. Mary had suffered a terrible death: she had been brutally raped and then assaulted with a vicious knife. So severe were her wounds that she had been almost disembowelled. The doctor who carried out the post-mortem suggested that death had taken place approximately a week before, presumably on the day she disappeared.

At his trial before Mr Justice Lawrence in January 1909, O'Connor told a remarkable story that an Irish navvy had killed Mary. The attacker had then wounded him as he tried in vain to save her. Although he was sporting wounds to support his story, the doctor who had examined O'Connor shortly after his arrest later testified that the wounds could easily have been self-inflicted.

Following conviction, O'Connor, a former soldier in the Durham Light Infantry, with a wife and three children living in Haswell, chose not to take advantage of the new appeal laws. He received just one visit while in the condemned cell, from his children on the day before his execution. He made no confession and went to the gallows without revealing the truth of what happened on that cold December night.

The story has one other, sad, footnote. On Wednesday 17 February 1909, there was a terrible pit disaster at West Stanley that left 148 men trapped below ground. Although a number were rescued, the accident claimed the lives of 114 miners. Among those that perished in the disaster was Thomas Donnelly, the father of the murdered girl.

32

THE CHOPWELL TRAGEDY

❖ *Abel Atherton, 8 December 1909* ❖

'Yer hanging an innocent man . . .'

(Last words spoken by Abel Atherton)

Two shots rang out. The first bullet flew harmlessly into the ground; the second embedded itself into the thigh of Mrs Elizabeth Patrick, fatally wounding her.

'Oh, my leg,' she cried, falling to the ground and, as her neighbour and 15-year-old daughter rushed to her aid, a man threw down the shotgun, rushed outside and tried for a moment to cut his own throat with a penknife. As a policeman approached, he handed over the knife and told him, 'I'm the man you want. She is quite dead . . . it's a bad job for me!'

Hangman Henry Pierrepoint. (Author's collection)

The story behind what became known as 'The Chopwell Tragedy' was told in court when Wigan-born miner Abel Atherton stood before Mr Justice Walton at Durham Assizes on 10 November 1909. Twenty-nine-year-old Atherton had left his native Lancashire several years before, and had been lodging at the home of Jacob and Elizabeth Patrick at Thames Street, Chopwell, near Gateshead.

He had been a pleasant, hard-working tenant who gave them no cause for concern until he developed an undesirable attraction towards his landlady's 15-year-old daughter, Frances. The young girl had initially been quite fond of Atherton but as his advances became more frequent and unwelcome, she complained to her parents and he was asked to leave the house. On Wednesday afternoon, 11 August 1909, Atherton returned to the house and accused Jacob Patrick of sexually abusing his own daughter. He was told to leave and it was made clear that he was no longer welcome. Atherton was unhappy at being unable to see the object of his desires and, returning to his new lodgings, he repeated his claims that she was having an incestuous relationship with her father. A short time later, he returned to Thames Street carrying a shotgun. He entered the house and, finding the whole family sitting at the kitchen table drinking tea with a neighbour, he pointed the gun. Mrs Patrick leaped to her feet and told him to get out of the house. She took hold of the barrel of the shotgun and manoeuvred it away as they struggled towards the kitchen door. Then the gun went off.

Atherton maintained that the shooting was an accident and that he had not intended to hurt anyone. He denied pointing the gun directly at Elizabeth Patrick or anyone else at the table, nor had he pulled the trigger. The gun had gone off accidentally and, as there was no intent to kill, his counsel offered a plea of guilty of manslaughter. The jury did not agree and Atherton was sentenced to death.

Throughout his stay in the condemned cell, Atherton was adamant that he was not guilty of murder. Even as he took the short walk to the gallows, he maintained his innocence. As Henry Pierrepoint placed the white cap over his head and reached for the lever, Atherton spoke for the last time.

33

DEAR TOMMY . . .

❖ *Thomas Craig, 12 July 1910* ❖

Dear Tommy,

Annie cannot answer anymore of your letters, and she has told me to tell you not to write to her again. She is soon to be married, and can now have nothing more to do with you.

(Letter written by Winifred Finn to Tommy Craig, 19 December 1909)

Annie Finn had fallen for the handsome Tommy Craig while he was stationed at Barnard Castle during his militia training. Although both were just in their teens, he 17, she a year younger, they soon fell in love and it was a love strong enough for her to accept that Craig was a 'bad 'un'. In the first twelve months of their courting he was in trouble for fighting, and in the following year he was arrested for housebreaking and causing grievous bodily harm when apprehended. It was while on bail pending this trial that he finally found himself in deep trouble.

Tommy Craig. (T.J. Leech archive)

Annie was horrified to find him charged with rape and he was subsequently sentenced to seven years' imprisonment, to be served at Portland Gaol. Nevertheless, she pledged to wait for him and wrote frequently as he counted the days until his release.

In the coming years, she remained true to her word until September 1909, when she met 22-year-old miner Thomas Henderson. It was love at first sight and, as she now had someone else occupying her thoughts, her letters to Craig grew less frequent until they stopped completely.

Craig suspected the worst. Annie was an attractive girl, and as he lay in his cell locked up for the night, he often feared that she might meet someone else. When the letters stopped, it confirmed his worst fears. He wrote reminding Annie of her promise to wait for him. When she failed to reply, he penned a further letter. Heavy with threats, it contained lines such as: 'Your happiness will be a short one. . . . I will forgive you if you are still Annie Finn, but if you are not it's God help you.' Then, a few days before Christmas 1909, he received a letter from Annie's sister Winifred.

In February 1910, Annie Finn married Thomas Henderson and they moved into a home at Carter's Yard, Oakwell Gate, Gateshead. It was to be only a short marriage. On Thursday 24 March, Craig was released from gaol under licence and immediately returned to the north-east. After a number of enquires, he found the lead he was looking for. On Saturday afternoon, he called at the house of Henderson's mother, introduced himself as an old friend of her new daughter-in-law and asked for their new address. She offered to show him and called at the house at Carter's Yard.

At first, Annie paid no attention to the stranger with her mother-in-law but when she finally looked at him, she smiled in recognition. 'You're Tommy Craig, aren't you?' she said, to which he replied, 'And you're Annie Finn.'

'No,' she replied, 'I'm Mrs Henderson now.'

Thomas Henderson had been standing on a chair, knocking a nail into the wall, and learning of the identity of the guest, he stepped down and offered his hand in friendship. Craig refused, turned to Annie and asked why she had not remained faithful. She told him truthfully that she preferred her new husband to him, at which Craig pulled out a revolver and began firing. The first shot hit Thomas Henderson, who staggered into the scullery and fell dead. The next two shots struck and wounded Annie, and then Craig pointed the gun at the dead man's mother.

'Oh, God. Spare me,' she cried, at which Craig fled from the house, making good his escape through the maze of narrow streets.

A manhunt was launched but Craig had gone to ground. A spate of housebreaking, in which food and drink were stolen, suggested that Craig was hiding in the area. Eventually, word reached detectives that a man had been seen sleeping in a hayloft at Dilston Cottage Farm. On 16 April, officers surrounded the barn and Craig was found asleep under a bale of hay. Still clutching the loaded gun, he gave himself up without a struggle.

At his murder trial on 25 June, Craig admitted that it had been his intention to kill the woman who had spurned him, and also Mr Justice Darling, who had sentenced him in 1905. Craig had been unable to find the address of the prominent judge and so had turned his attention first to Annie Henderson. He claimed that the killing of Thomas Henderson was unintentional; he had meant only to wound Henderson, who had provoked him by marrying the woman he had loved and lost.

34

WITH NECESSARY INTENT?

❖ *Robert Upton, 24 March 1914* ❖

There had been two men in Elizabeth Burden's life. For over two years, she had been involved with both Robert Upton and Charles Gribben, working initially as housekeeper, but in both cases the relationships had developed from business to one of a more romantic nature. Upton and Gribben had much in common: both worked as labourers and lived in the same part of Jarrow, and both were fond of spending Saturday night getting drunk together in local pubs. Elizabeth divided her time between the two men, spending the first part of the week with Gribben and the latter with Upton.

Then Mrs Burden dropped a bombshell. She told them both she was leaving the area with another man, Jack Bloy, whom she intended to marry. Upton in particular was distraught. In a jealous rage, he told her that she would not have Bloy, nor for that matter Gribben.

Ten days later, on Saturday 20 December, after spending the night drinking, Upton and his son Joe returned with Gribben to the latter's home, where they continued drinking before finally retiring for the night. In the early hours Joe Upton woke to find his father attacking Gribben with a razor. He tried in vain to stop his father but was unable to prevent Upton committing a brutal cutthroat murder on the sleeping Gribben. Upton then turned the razor on himself. The police were called and Upton told the first officer at the scene, 'I have killed the bastard, I done it, let me die.'

His trial before Mr Justice Ridley at Durham Assizes was brief. The chief witness for the prosecution was the former housekeeper, recently married and now known as

Hangman John Ellis. (Crime Picture Archive)

Elizabeth Bloy. She told the court of the threats he had made to her, and both Gribben and her new husband. There was no doubt that Upton was drunk when he committed the crime, but there was an apparent lack of motive. Why had he chosen to kill his former friend? It was clear that there was jealousy between them but it was Bloy who had stolen the heart of the woman he loved, not Gribben, and Upton had long been aware that he had been sharing the affections of the former Mrs Burden.

His counsel pressed for a verdict of manslaughter, claiming that Upton was not guilty of murder as he was too drunk to form the necessary intent. It failed to save Upton from the gallows. His execution marked the first visit of John Ellis as principal hangman at the gaol.

35

THE CONFESSOR

❖ Frank Steele, 11 August 1915 ❖

Frank Steele had already confessed to several people that he had 'done Nan in', and when word reached the local police, they hurried to investigate. Forcing their way into the room that Steele shared with Nora 'Nana' Barrett, they discovered a gruesome sight. Twenty-one-year-old Nana lay dead, her throat cut from ear to ear, a bloodstained razor lying nearby.

By the late spring of 1915, Steele and Barrett had been living together for about three months at 31 Nelson Street, Gateshead, but Nana had since met another man, Joe Bell, and their relationship had cooled. Steele soon found out Bell had been visiting Nana while he was at work and when he discovered a love letter written by Nana to Bell, he was overcome with jealousy and began to drink heavily.

On the early afternoon of Sunday 16 May, a neighbour noticed Nana standing at her front door. The same neighbour spotted Steele there at around 1.30 p.m., hastily locking the door and leaving the house in darkness with the blinds drawn.

Later that afternoon, Steele bumped into a number of friends in the town centre and all later said he appeared to be much the worse for drink. To more than one, Steele had announced that he had murdered Nana but, because he was in such a drunken state, none of them believed him. Neither did Steele's mother when he visited her that same afternoon, but when he returned the next day in a sober state and confessed again to his mother, this time she feared the worst and contacted the local police.

Tried before Mr Justice Ridley in July, 28-year-old Steele claimed that he had no motive for the murder. His counsel maintained that the correct verdict should be one of manslaughter, as the accused had been too drunk to form any intent or be aware of his actions.

Evidence was shown of his jealousy at his former sweetheart's relationship with Joe Bell. This, together with the testimony of the neighbour who saw him coolly lock up and leave the house shortly after the time that doctors had estimated for the death, was enough to show otherwise. It took the jury just two hours to find that Steele was not incapacitated by drink and had a motive for the crime, and he was duly found guilty of the wilful murder of Nana Barrett.

36

AN AXE FOR THE LADY, A RAZOR FOR ME

❖ *Joseph Deans, 20 December 1916* ❖

From the first time he met Catherine Convery, a widow from Monkwearmouth, Sunderland, 44-year-old Joseph Deans had been very possessive of her. After spending seventeen years working as a gold miner in South Africa, Deans had returned to his native north-east in the summer of 1915 a wealthy man. He soon fell in love with Mrs Convery and began to lavish money and gifts on her.

In early October 1916, his world was shattered when he discovered that she was also involved with another man. On hearing the news, he rushed round to her house and accused her of two-timing him. Picking up a knife from the table, he shouted, 'I will do it now,' as she cowered alongside her terrified daughter.

A few days later, Deans tried to buy a gun but was refused as he did not have a licence. On the morning of 7 October, clutching a picture of Catherine, he told a friend, 'I love every hair on her head but I'm going to finish her off tonight.'

Just a few hours later, another friend saw Deans holding a strange-shaped parcel. Asked what he was carrying, Deans calmly said, 'An axe for the lady, a razor for me.' As with his previous boasts and threats, his friends did not take them seriously. Later that evening, Deans was drinking in the Grey Horse pub, leaving a little before closing time, much the worse for wear. As he left the bar, he was heard to mutter, 'I will do it tonight.'

Not long after Deans had departed, drinkers were horrified to see Mrs Convery stagger into the same pub, blood pouring from a long wound to the head, crying, 'He's murdered me this time.' Despite horrific wounds to her head and neck, with the help of friends from the pub she managed to walk to the nearby local hospital.

Deans was arrested in his lodging after he made a failed attempt to cut his own throat. Charged with attempted murder and attempted suicide, he was remanded into Durham Gaol. Six days later, Mrs Convery died from her wounds in hospital. Deans was now charged with murder and indicted to appear at the next Assizes.

On 15 November, when he stood before Mr Justice Low, his defence was insanity. The prosecution claimed that it was murder fuelled by jealousy and rage; he had spent over £100 on the murdered woman since returning to Sunderland, and when she began to two-time him he lost his temper. The jury needed just five minutes to return a verdict of guilty. Asked if he had anything to say before sentence was passed, Deans shouted, 'I killed the woman and I'm pleased I killed her.'

37

FOR SHE WAS A DEAD WRONG WOMAN

❖ *William Hall, 23 March 1920* ❖

Customers in Sunderland's Tynemouth Castle pub who saw pensioner William Hall, a 66-year-old brass worker, and his companion Mary Dixon, a widow some fifteen years younger, assumed that they were just a normal couple enjoying a quiet night out. What they did not know was that Hall had decided that later that night he would carry out his threat to kill the woman with whom he was sharing a drink. With no family of her own, Mary Dixon had lived with Hall sporadically for close on two years, until finally, in September 1919, she told him she had found work as a night attendant at a lodging house in Grey Street, Sunderland. She also told him that it was the end of their romance. Hall took the news badly and, on the afternoon of 5 November, told his sister who lived with him that he was going to see Mary the following day to try to get her to change her mind and to come back to him.

At 6 p.m. he called at her lodgings and, after a short conversation, Mary picked up her hat and coat and accompanied him to the public house. They were seen enjoying a drink and returned to Hall's house later that night. Hall's sister heard them talking in his room at around 10 p.m. and they seemed to be on pleasant terms, with no raised voices or shouting.

On the following morning the sister noticed his blinds drawn and assumed that he had persuaded Mary to rekindle their romance and that she had stayed the night. She left the house, and when she returned at around lunchtime there was still no sign of movement from her brother's room. She tried to attract attention by knocking on his door and asking if they wanted a cup of tea, but received no reply. She knocked again a short time later and this time she tried the door. It was locked. Receiving no reply, she hurried out into the street and located a policeman. Entry was forced, and there on the bed lay William Hall and Mary Dixon; both had gaping throat wounds. Although Hall was still alive, Mary lay dead in a pool of blood.

Hall was taken to hospital, where he recovered from his injuries to face a charge of murder. He had already confessed to the police that he had killed Mary, and when he appeared in court before Mr Justice Bailache on 4 March 1920, he pleaded guilty under provocation.

The court heard how Hall had spent the evening with Mary at the Tynemouth Castle public house, and she had agreed to accompany him back at closing time. He had by now formed the impression that she had agreed to his request to abandon plans to end their relationship and to take up the position at the lodging house. To his dismay, when he invited her to stay the night, she refused, telling him she intended returning to Grey Street. This, he claimed, was enough provocation and he had picked up his razor and killed her, before turning it on himself.

The prosecution claimed that it was another case of a lover spurned. They called witnesses who testified that Hall had threatened to kill Mary in the past and that he had told another neighbour that he was meeting Mary that night. In the neighbour's presence, Hall had made a chilling gesture of drawing his finger across his throat.

Asked if he had anything to say before the death sentence was passed upon him, Hall replied, 'If there was nothing gained in what I did, I can stand under God and say there was nothing lost, for she was a dead wrong woman.'

38

THE OLD SOLDIER

❖ *James Riley, 30 November 1920* ❖

James Riley bit his lip hard as he heard sentence of death passed over him. Although he had often cursed that he would 'swing for her', now that he stood convicted of the murder of his wife, the reality of the situation hit home.

Fifty-one-year-old Riley had been too old to be called up during the latter days of the war, when the country's very future hung in the balance, but despite his age – he was 49 at the time – he had volunteered for duties and had seen action in both India and Greece, where he was taken ill, contracting malaria.

By the autumn of 1920, James Riley and his wife Mary had been married for over twenty years. Theirs was a tempestuous relationship. No stranger to the police, Riley had been warned numerous times about his behaviour when, on Saturday 2 October, police once more called at Riley's house. Mary told them that her husband had come home drunk and tried to pick yet another quarrel. When she failed to rise to the bait, he began to beat her, and her cries alerted the neighbours. Although the police calmed him down, in their presence he was heard to make threats that he would kill her. 'I'll swing for you Mary, I swear I will,' he shouted.

Just seven days later, on 9 October, Riley finally carried out his threat. In the early hours, he knocked on a neighbour's door and told them that he had killed his wife. He asked them to give him a chance to escape and not to notify the police for one hour. As Riley made off across nearby fields, they went to check if his story was true, and finding Mary Riley battered to death in her bed, they went to contact the police. Riley was picked up before sunrise.

He pleaded not guilty to murder but guilty to manslaughter at his trial before Mr Justice Swift. He tried to pass the blame on to his wife, claiming that she had been drinking heavily and had tried to start a fight with him. Riley said he tried to push her away and she fell heavily to the floor. They had exchanged further blows and he left her on the floor when he retired to bed. It was not until he awoke in the early hours that he realised she was dead.

His counsel argued that, since Riley had not intended to commit murder, he was guilty only of manslaughter. The prosecution pointed to his past behaviour and produced evidence from officers in front of whom he had made threats to kill his wife shortly before she was found dead.

As Riley awaited his fate in the condemned cell, local miners organised a petition for his reprieve. Although over 32,000 signatures were collected, it did not save the old soldier from making an eight o'clock appointment with his executioners.

39

DELAYED IN THE POST

❖ James Williamson, 21 March 1922 ❖

The war had left James Williamson with a painful disability. Badly wounded when he was shot in both legs at Salonica, he was thenceforward to suffer from a permanent limp. The war hero returned to hard times. Finding work in the mines, he settled with his wife, Mary, and five children at Easington. By the end of 1921, relations between Williamson and his wife had all but broken down, and in December she left him, taking the children with her to her parents' house in Houghton-le-Spring. A week before Christmas, she obtained a separation order on the grounds of his ill treatment.

When he learned that she had been awarded 30s a week maintenance, Williamson was incensed. He had been hoping for reconciliation but her actions now seemed to signal the end of these hopes. His bitterness at the separation order and maintenance award led him to make threats against his wife.

He visited Mary on 29 December, and when he was invited to stay for the New Year celebrations, it seemed his hopes of a reunited family may be coming true. As he was due back in work, he returned home on 2 January 1922, where he had posted the first of his maintenance payments to his wife. On the following day he was invited back to Houghton-le-Spring at the weekend and, after finishing work for the week, he rejoined his wife.

On the Saturday morning Mary asked Williamson where the maintenance money that he owed her was. He told her that he had posted it a few days before, but when the cheque failed to arrive in the morning post a fierce quarrel broke out. She accused him of lying and not sending the money as promised. He insisted that he had posted the money but still she refused to believe him. Suddenly he leaped to his feet and, pulling out his razor, he lashed at Mary's throat in full view of two of their children, who rushed from the house. Returning with a neighbour, they found their father kneeling over his wife, hacking away at her throat with the razor. By the time he was dragged from the stricken woman, her head had been almost severed.

Williamson offered a defence of insanity when he appeared before Mr Justice Bray on 1 March. The jury needed just five minutes to find that he was sane, and once sentence was passed, Williamson saluted the judge and said, 'Thank you, sir.' The cheque that Mary Williamson had doubted her husband had posted arrived on the Monday morning after the murder.

40

THE UNINVITED GUEST

❖ Daniel Cassidy, 3 April 1923 ❖

The party to welcome in the New Year of 1923 was in full swing and drink was flowing merrily when the door of a house in Woodbine Street, Hendon, Sunderland suddenly burst open and in strode an angry man. Pointing a gun above the heads of the revellers, he let off a shot. Then, lowering the weapon, he fired four more times before he was overpowered and bundled out into the street. Inside was carnage: two people had been seriously wounded, while another lay dead.

Shotgun killer Daniel Cassidy. (T.J. Leech archive)

Events leading up to the tragedy could be traced back to the autumn of the previous year, when 60-year-old blacksmith Daniel Cassidy and his wife Elizabeth had parted after many years of marriage. She went home to her native Dublin but returned to Sunderland for Christmas.

The Woodbine Street house was the home of Agnes Hodgson, one of the Cassidy's married daughters. All the members of the family had been invited to the party, with just one exception. Cassidy lived on the same street with another of his daughters, and when she left to go to the party he brooded over it before picking up his gun and crossing the street.

At just after seven o'clock that evening the uninvited guest made his entrance and began his murderous attack. His daughter Elizabeth Quinn and his wife Elizabeth were both wounded, but his son-in-law Bernard Quinn, who had been entertaining the guests, playing the melodeon, was fatally wounded.

At his trial before Mr Justice Roche in February, Cassidy said that he blamed his wife for what had happened; she had been trying to turn his family against him, and it was at her request that he had not been invited to the party. He claimed that he had gone across the street with the intention of trying to break up the gathering, such was his anger at being snubbed. He had not intended to shoot anyone, much less kill them. Realising the consequence of his actions, he had planned to then turn the gun on himself, but was thwarted when he was overpowered.

Cassidy's defence counsel suggested that he was insane at the time of the shooting and told the court that he had spent some time in an asylum before the war. The prosecution disputed the claims of insanity and said that, although Cassidy had indeed spent time in the mental hospital, it had been under observation as a voluntary patient, and after less than a fortnight he was discharged. Doctors there claimed that he had shown no signs of insanity. They also alleged that when he heard he was not to be invited to the party, he had issued threats. On New Year's Eve he had spoken to his daughter Agnes and said, 'Tell the bitch she is looking for trouble.' This, the prosecution claimed, showed that there was a degree of premeditation, and, agreeing with this version of events, the jury took just a short time to return a guilty verdict.

41

THE HAND THAT FIRED THE GUN

❖ Hassan Muhamed, 8 August 1923 ❖

It was to be her second marriage. Her first husband had died in the previous year and her new husband-to-be, Hassan Muhamed, a 33-year-old ship's fireman, was, like her first, an Arab seaman. Jane Nagi, aged 25, worked in a café on East Holborn, South Shields. On the afternoon of Monday 12 March 1923, two days before she was due to walk down the aisle for the second time, she arrived at work drunk and was told she was unfit for duty. She told her boss she was waiting for Muhamed and, when he turned up at 4 p.m., a fierce quarrel broke out between them.

Jane told Muhamed she no longer wished to marry him and, as tempers rose, she swore at Muhamed, slapped his face and scratched at his throat. So heated did the row become that the police were called. Both were cautioned and warned that they would face charges if they did not cease their quarrel.

As Jane stood in the doorway, Muhamed went into the kitchen. When he emerged, he asked Jane if she was serious about ending their relationship. She told him that she was, and in a rage Muhamed

Hassan Muhamed in court. (T.J. Leech archive)

The café where Jane Nagi was murdered. (T.J. Leech archive)

stormed out of the restaurant. Minutes later, he returned and saw that Jane was still in the kitchen. Suddenly, without warning, he pulled out a revolver and fired once, hitting Jane in the breast, killing her instantly.

When he stood trial for murder before Lord Chief Justice Hewart in July, Muhamed gave a very different version of the events that day. He said that when he arrived at the café he had found his fiancée sitting on the knee of Sam Ali, who worked there as a cook. They began to quarrel, which ended with Muhamed and Ali rolling around in a fight. As Muhamed gained the upper hand, Ali pulled out a gun. During the disturbance, the gun went off and the bullet struck and killed Jane Nagi. Muhamed then overpowered him. Realising the implications of what happened, Ali and the others at the café tried to frame Muhamed, devising a story between them that put the blame squarely on him.

The prosecution's version of events was that, upset at the break-up of his relationship, Muhamed had left the café only to return a short time later with a revolver. The jury chose to believe it was the hand of Muhamed that had fired the gun, killing Jane Nagi just two days before she was due to become his bride.

42

THE FATAL NOTE

❖ *Matthew Frederick Atkinson Nunn, 2 January 1924* ❖

'This is the end. Think kindly of me. Tell Mrs Kelly I am sorry. This is the only way out. I can stand it no longer.'

(Note to his mother by Matthew Nunn, 12 September 1923)

When 24-year-old Matthew Nunn learned that he was going to be a father, he was delighted at the news and wasted no time in asking his girlfriend's parents for permission to marry. Receiving their blessing, he hurried to tell Minetta Mary Kelly that they could now begin to make wedding plans. There was, however, one slight problem.

Minetta and Nunn had been courting for just over a year, and the 20-year-old had taken the news of her falling pregnant with rather less enthusiasm than the prospective father. Not only did she not feel ready for motherhood, unbeknown to Nunn she also had another lover and, not wanting to commit to a relationship with just one man, she told Nunn that she had no wish to be married. She also began to cool on the relationship with Nunn and he took this state of affairs badly. The anger he felt at the rejection was compounded when he discovered that she had another boyfriend, who, when he learned that she was pregnant, also proposed marriage.

On the night of Tuesday 11 September 1923, Minetta and Nunn left his home at Tantobie, Tanfield, County Durham to visit a local public house. At two o'clock the following morning, Nunn knocked at a neighbour's house and, when the door was opened, he stumbled inside and slumped to the floor with blood oozing from his badly gashed throat. Nunn was unable to speak and managed to scribble a note saying that 'Min' had done this to him. Police officers soon elicited more information from the wounded man and made their way to nearby Bushfields, where they discovered the body of Minetta. In her lap was a bloodstained razor.

Nunn recovered from his injuries in due course. Although he steadfastly maintained that Minetta had committed suicide after first attacking him, his story was not believed and it was left to the jury at Durham Assizes to decide his fate.

On 14 November 1923, Nunn appeared before Mr Justice McCardle. Asked to explain how it was that a razor belonging to Nunn's father had caused the fatal wounds, he said that Minetta had asked to borrow one on behalf of her father, as his was being repaired. After leaving the public house, Minetta had taken the razor from him to loan to her father. As they walked home, they began to quarrel and she then struck out at him, cutting his throat before turning the razor on herself.

The prosecution counsel pointed out that there were a number of inconsistencies in Nunn's story. First, while Nunn's injuries were comparatively slight – he had made a full recovery in the two months since the attack – Minetta's head was almost severed. The pathologist who had carried out the post-mortem told the court that it was impossible for a suicide to produce such horrific self-inflicted wounds. Secondly and most damning was a note that Nunn had left on the table at the neighbour's house after collapsing through the door. Addressed to his mother, it was effectively a confession to murder. It took the jury fifty minutes to reach their verdict, that the fatal note left by Nunn amounted to a confession, and duly find him guilty as charged. Following the rejection of his appeal, Nunn spent Christmas in the condemned cell, with his execution scheduled to take place on Wednesday 2 January 1924.

The chaplain who sat with Nunn in his final moments later made a complaint about the execution and the conduct of hangman Thomas Pierrepoint:

> I was with Nunn in the M.O.'s room in the reception ward when at a few moments to eight the door was pushed open without any preliminary knock and the executioners burst into the room. (I can describe the entrance in no milder words.) The executioner pinioned Nunn's hands and although I asked him to wait until I had put my surplice on (it was in my hands at the time), he took no notice, seized Nunn by the arm and pushed him out of the room and the procession started. . . . I have been present at a number of executions and never have I witnessed such callous haste.

43

A LIFE FOR A LIFE

❖ *Henry Graham, 15 April 1925* ❖

Window cleaner Henry Graham was adamant that he was not going to pay. In the summer of 1924, 42-year-old Graham and his 30-year-old wife Margaret split up. Taking their adopted son, Margaret went to live with her mother in Rutland Street, Sunderland. A few weeks later, Graham's estranged wife obtained a separation order against him, resulting in him being required to pay 15*s* a week. Graham received notice of the terms of the order and a demand for the first payment a few days before Christmas.

On Sunday 21 December, Margaret visited her sister Elizabeth, a long-term patient in Sunderland Infirmary. Accompanied by her sister's husband, Robert Doleman, and a cousin, she left the infirmary at 3.15 p.m., buoyed up with the news that Elizabeth had been told she would be discharged and home by Christmas.

They had hardly left the hospital grounds when Henry Graham approached. 'I want an explanation!' he shouted, holding out the letter. Margaret stopped to speak to him, while the two men walked on out of earshot and waited for her to finish. Graham and his wife spoke for almost fifteen minutes and their voices began to rise. Suddenly he lashed out and struck Margaret in the face, knocking her to the ground. As she fell, Graham took out a knife, dropped to his knees and stabbed her several times in the back.

Henry Graham. (Author's collection)

Seeing what was happening, Doleman raced back and tried to intervene, only for Graham to point the knife, threatening him if he came closer. Doleman turned and ran to find a policeman, while Graham fled, wielding the knife at the crowd that had gathered. As he made his escape, several gave chase, the crowd baying for his blood, and he was tackled to the ground and detained until police arrived on the scene. Graham travelled in the ambulance with his wife to the same infirmary she had recently attended as a visitor, where she died from her injuries on arrival.

Graham appeared before Mr Justice Acton at Durham Assizes on 6 March. His defence was insanity based on injuries he had sustained during the war. The prosecution presented a case of wilful murder done through rage at having to pay maintenance, and anger at her refusal to return to him.

Graham thanked the jury after sentence of death was passed: 'I am heartily satisfied at the verdict. I guess it's a life for a life.'

'I can die happy now,' Graham said after being visited on the day before his execution by his adopted son. Assistant hangman William Willis later recalled the case in his diary:

> Sat reading the Bible and smoking a cigarette at eight o'clock at night. He had complained of the way in which he had been treated in prison, and the Governor told him he had been treated all right.
>
> Hefty chap, clean shaven and smart. Came along to scaffold chanting: 'Oh Lamb of God, I come.' Death inst.

DOUBLE EXECUTION.

Men Hanged Side by Side at Durham.

FATE MET WITH COMPOSURE.

Coroner Graham's Criticism of Capital Punishment.

A double execution took place in Durham Gaol this morning, when Thomas Henry Shelton, aged 25, fitter, of Gateshead, and Henry Graham, aged 42, window cleaner, of Sunderland, suffered the extreme penalty of the law for sweetheart and wife murder, respectively.

Both men walked with steady steps to the scaffold, and last night Graham told some friends that he was "as happy as a skylark."

Conducting the inquests, Mr. John Graham, the veteran Coroner, delivered a strong criticism of capital punishment, and advocated as an alternative penalty, imprisonment for life, without any remission of sentence.

It is 17 years since two men were hanged together at Durham, and on that occasion the murderers were J. T. Noble and Robert Lawman, both of Gateshead.

Newspaper headline recording the double execution in 1925. (T.J. Leech archive)

44

THE BREAK-UP

❖ *Thomas Henry Shelton, 15 April 1925* ❖

'Dear Tom,
It must be plain to you that things have not been as they should be for some considerable time, and it has therefore come to this: that in the interests of both of us we should part.'
(Extract from letter written by Ruth Rodgers, January 1925)

The relationship between Thomas Shelton and Ruth Surtees Rodgers changed when she found work as a confidential clerk at the offices of the City Floorcloth and Linoleum Company on Pink Lane, Newcastle, in the autumn of 1924. Before she took up the job,

Ruth Rodgers. (T.J. Leech archive)

the pair, both 25, had been engaged for four years, but had been courting for over six. Her family had never really taken to Gateshead-born Shelton, who, although always immaculately dressed, seemed to drift in and out of work as a mechanical engineer, and Ruth gradually began to realise that the relationship had now all but run its course.

Shelton was unaware of her feelings but had noticed a change in her behaviour. He began looking for clues to the change and decided that it was linked to her new job. Ruth's office manager was 45-year-old married father of three Walter Shiel. In December 1924 Shelton began to suspect that Shiel was more than just her boss. In some ways this was true. Ruth had lost her father at a young age and began to look up to the kindly Shiel, twenty years her senior, as a father figure.

Shelton's jealousy led to arguments between them and he started to write her abusive letters. Ruth confided in Shiel that she was frightened of her fiancé and, unaware that he was the cause of Shelton's jealousy, he offered to escort her home. Shelton was waiting outside the office when he saw her climb into Shiel's car. Now he was convinced that they were having an affair.

On the afternoon of 29 January 1925, he paid a visit to a private detective, John Trotter, a former policeman, and asked him to investigate whether Ruth was being unfaithful. He produced a number of letters, gave a few personal details about her and, having satisfied Trotter that he had the means to pay his fees, made an appointment for the following afternoon. Shelton was not to keep this second appointment.

Later that same day, Ruth's sister Eleanor heard a loud knocking on the front door and opened it to find her sister lying on the front doorstep, bleeding from a horrific throat wound. 'Mrs Rodgers, I have done her in,' shouted Shelton from the middle of the street, before he stumbled across to a neighbour's house and collapsed from his own self-inflicted neck injuries.

By the time the doctor arrived, Ruth Rodgers had died from her injuries. Shelton's wounds were found to be superficial and, after hospital treatment, he was deemed well enough to face a charge of murder. At his Durham Assizes trial before Mr Justice Acton on 6 March, Shelton's counsel tried to plead for manslaughter caused by the intense jealousy he felt at losing his fiancée.

Walter Shiel, who had since made a failed suicide attempt and lost his job through the scandal of being linked with the murder, maintained that there had been nothing going on between him and Ruth, and that Shelton had no grounds for being jealous. Counsel then tried to show that Shelton's elated and exuberant behaviour after his arrest suggested that he was insane.

The prosecution pointed out that there was no history of insanity in the family and that Shelton had made threats against Ruth on many occasions prior to her murder. Witnesses to the attack testified that he had chased her into the road before cutting her throat. This showed that there was premeditation as Shelton had caught hold of Ruth after she managed to escape the first attack.

With the sentence of death passed on him, as Shelton was led from the dock he pointed to the man he blamed for the break-up of his once-happy relationship, shouting, 'That's the man, Shiel's the trouble!' Shelton's mother died while he was awaiting the gallows, just days before a petition containing thousands of signatures was ignored by the Home Secretary, who announced that, in the case of Thomas Shelton, the law must take its course.

45

THE JEALOUS MAN

❖ *James Smith, 10 August 1926* ❖

Twenty-three-year-old ship's fireman James Smith and his wife Catherine had been married for only a little over a year and already they had parted three times. There was a simple reason for these break-ups: Smith was a very jealous man. They had wed in January 1925. Catherine, three years his senior, had been married once before and already had two young children.

Smith took to his new family but whenever he got drunk, which was often, he used to become jealous about her past relationships. Although she tried to help control his jealousy, she was unable to do so and her only way out seemed to be to leave. Three times she walked out, and three times he persuaded her that he would change his ways. In February 1926, they parted for the fourth, and what would be the last, time. As before, she returned to her parents' home in Silver Street, Newcastle.

Catherine's mother, Mrs Scott, owned another house on Silver Street, which was tenanted by a number of families and single workmen. She made it her business to keep the house respectable and when, on 18 April, she called to collect rent and saw a number of men gambling, including her son-in-law, James Smith, she called the police. Smith was enraged, and on the following morning he and a number of other men assembled outside

Mrs Scott's house and began making threats against her. When she threatened to call the police, the men dispersed but, as they did so, Smith made a number of threats.

Later that afternoon, Smith's wife and mother-in-law were alone in the house when Smith called round. As he and his wife talked upstairs, her younger sister returned home. Moments later, a scream rang out and Smith was seen dragging his wife, bleeding heavily from a stab wound to her breast, down the stairs. The police were summoned and Smith made no attempt to flee. He went outside into the street and handed a knife to a friend, asking him to give it to a policeman. 'You can do it yourself,' his friend said, gesturing to the constable who was hurrying up the street. Smith handed the knife over and submitted to arrest without a struggle.

James Smith pleaded insanity when he stood before Mr Justice Wright on 2 July. His defence claimed that he had contracted malaria while on naval service in Mesopotamia and had made a number of failed suicide attempts.

Asked if he had anything to say before sentence of death was passed, Smith made the same statement he had made when first arrested and at each subsequent court hearing: 'I am not guilty, sir. I did not know what I was doing.' Smith pulled out a photograph of his wife and children and gazed at it intently as the judge condemned him to death. 'Amen,' he shouted, as the judge finished the dreaded words.

46

A FAKED SUICIDE

❖ *John Thomas Dunn, 6 January 1928* ❖

At first hearing it had seemed a plausible story. In the early hours of Sunday 25 September 1927, neighbours in Lumsdons Buildings, Sacriston, County Durham woke to shouts of 'Help! Call the police!' Moments later, 52-year-old John Dunn rushed out and shouted that his wife had killed herself. The police were called and, entering the kitchen, they found the body of 44-year-old Ada Dunn near the back door of her house. She was dead and there were marks around her neck, presumably made by the length of rope hanging from a metal peg attached to the kitchen wall. Dunn said that he had cut her down and removed the noose but, unable to revive her, he had run for help.

Initially, his story was accepted, but while neighbours began to offer their condolences, at the local hospital the police surgeon soon found something that was to trigger a murder inquiry. Forensic tests found bruises around the neck inconsistent with hanging; they were not in the place where they would be expected to be. When measurements were made of the rope, they found that if Ada Dunn had been hanged as her husband claimed, her feet would have touched the floor!

Dunn's behaviour also aroused suspicion. While officers examined the house, Dunn stood in the yard cracking jokes with neighbours – hardly the behaviour of a bereaved and grieving husband. Questioned as to why his wife would want to take her own life, Dunn claimed that she had often spoken of suicide. He said that they had been sleeping in separate rooms that night, and when he had woken in the early hours of the morning, he discovered her hanging.

Investigations soon prompted a different picture of events. Police learned that on 13 September, Ada Dunn had left her husband after disagreements over financial matters. He had persuaded her to return, which she did on 24 September. There were also the alleged suicide threats. No one other than Dunn had heard her make such statements, and their young sons both told detectives that shortly before her death they had heard their parents fighting. The final proof, if any was needed, was letters found in her room, written by Dunn and dated days before the murder. In them, he wrote begging her to come home but made threats against her if she refused.

Dunn, a former inmate at Winterton Asylum, was tried at Durham Assizes before Mr Justice Roche on 15 November 1927. He pleaded insanity, but the case against him, that he had committed a brutal murder which he then tried to disguise as suicide, convinced the jury of his guilt.

47

THE TALL MAN

Norman Elliott, 10 August 1928

The large, brass paperweight crashed through the window and landed on the pavement. As passers-by stopped to see what had caused the sudden disturbance, a tall man turned up his raincoat and hurried down the street. It was close to 3 p.m. on the afternoon of Thursday 16 February 1928 and, curious as to what had caused the heavy object to land in the road, a number of men entered the premises of the Ferryhill Black Bull branch of Lloyds Bank and discovered cashier William Byland Abbey lying fatally wounded. Abbey was able to say that he had been the victim of a robbery and had been battered several times about the head before being stabbed twice in the neck.

'Who did it?' asked one of the men as the police were summoned.

'A tall man,' he muttered weakly. 'He's just left.' As others set off in pursuit of the attacker, someone made the stricken man comfortable, trying vainly to stem the flow of blood. Within minutes, Abbey succumbed to his injuries and slumped to the ground. Beside the body lay a vicious, black-handled cobbler's knife.

It had been the second robbery ending in murder at a branch of Lloyds Bank in recent years. Four years earlier, a cashier had been killed in similar circumstances while cashing up

Mr. Norman Elliott. Durham County Asylum, Winterton, Ferryhill

in account with

Lloyds Bank Limited,

Durham.

Moneys in this account bear interest and are subject to 14 days notice when withdrawn.

NO PAYMENT WILL BE MADE EXCEPT ON PRODUCTION OF THIS BOOK.

DATE.		PARTICULARS.	DEBIT.			CREDIT.			BALANCE.		
1926 Dec	3	Trustee Deps				47	12	6	47	12	6
		Birth certificate		3	7				47	8	11
	7	Self	10						37	8	11
	24	do	10						27	8	11
1927 Jan	13	do	7						20	8	11
Feb	4	Cash				38			58	8	11
			27	3	7	85	12	6			

Norman Elliott's account book at Lloyds Bank. (Author's collection)

in a one-man branch in Hampshire. In that case, the killer was soon brought to justice and executed at Winchester Prison. There had been talk at the time of stopping the practice of having lone clerks staffing the banks, and even of arming them with revolvers, but neither idea had been taken on board and things had reverted to normal.

Missing from the bank was over £200 and police soon had a strong lead. A bus conductress told them that at 3.50 p.m. on 16 February, a man she recognised by sight had boarded her bus. Earlier that day, she had seen him in Ferryhill, and when she light-heartedly reprimanded him for ignoring her, he bluntly denied being in Ferryhill that day. Aware that the robbery had taken place minutes before he had boarded her bus, she felt this a little suspicious. Although she did not know his name, she knew he worked as a nurse at the Durham County Asylum, in Sedgefield.

Detectives were soon interviewing 23-year-old Norman Elliott. Elliott, an account holder at Lloyds Bank, had married his heavily pregnant wife Elizabeth just a month earlier, and as they were unable to afford their own home, he was living at the hospital while she lived with her parents at the Turk's Head public house in Kelloe. Enquiries found that before the murder Elliott was having financial problems, but on the day after, he had paid almost £20 in cash for some furniture and carpets.

Norman Elliott. (T.J. Leech archive)

FERRYHILL BANK MURDER.

MAN ARRESTED AND CHARGED.

The police yesterday arrested a man at Kelloe, Durham, and subsequently charged him with the murder of William Byland Abbey at the Ferryhill branch of Lloyds Bank on February 16.

The arrest was made by Superintendent Foster (who has been conducting the investigations), Inspector Walker, and Detective Hedley.

The man, Norman Elliott, was brought before the Mayor of Durham at the police station and remanded until February 29.

Upwards of 6,000 people attended the funeral yesterday of Mr. Abbey. The service was held at the war memorial in the village, being conducted by the Rev. F. Rowland Pearson, former pastor at Ferryhill Baptist Church, with which Mr. Abbey had been identified for a number of years. The chief mourners were the Misses Abbey, his three sisters, and Mr. J. B. Abbey, Mr. E. V. Abbey, and Mr. C. H. Abbey, his brothers. Representatives of Lloyds Bank and of the Durham Cathedral Choristers' Association were present.

A press cutting showing the arrest of Elliott and the funeral of William Abbey. (Author's collection)

Elliott was taken in for questioning. Officers who searched his quarters found almost £150 in notes, some bloodstained. He was formally charged on 20 February, while a few miles away the funeral of William Abbey took place.

At his trial at Durham Assizes before Mr Justice McKinnon on 27 June, Elliott readily admitted his part in the robbery but claimed that he had an accomplice, a compulsive gambler named Sinclair, and it was he who had killed the clerk. He said he had arranged to meet Sinclair at the bank at closing time. Explaining the bloodstains found on his clothing and on the notes, Elliott said he had arrived first, gone inside and asked Abbey if a man had been in asking for him. When Abbey replied that no one had been enquiring for him, Elliott left, to return a few moments later. Now he found the doors closed. A bloodstained Sinclair then appeared at the door, dragged him inside and thrust a handful of money at him.

Several witnesses had identified Elliott and in each case they said he was alone. Nobody had seen a bloodstained second man anywhere near the bank that afternoon. Elliott also added that he knew Abbey, as they both lived in Spennymoor, and if he had indeed been the attacker, Abbey would have identified him instead of claiming that the killer was 'a tall man'.

The prosecuting counsel, G.B. Mortimer, told the court that, while it was true that both men lived in the same town, they only had Elliott's word that the two had ever met before 16 February. None of Abbey's friends or family were aware of any such friendship.

'Oh, Mother! Mother! Mother!' Elliott cried, as he was found guilty and sentenced to death, his screams being clearly heard as he was carried away to the cells under the courtroom. He became a father for the first time as he awaited the hangman, and once his appeal was rejected he spent his last days on earth gazing in tears at the photograph of his wife and new son, whom she had named Norman in memory of his father, the tall man he would never know.

48

THE GRANDSON

❖ Charles Conlin, 4 January 1929 ❖

On Saturday evening, 22 September 1928, Charlie Conlin called at the home of his grandparents and told them that his mother had been taken ill. He asked them to accompany him back to his home at Norton, a small village near Stockton, and, agreeing to his request, they climbed into his Austin 7 car.

On the following morning, a gardener in search of fresh soil for her plants at Briar Garth made a gruesome discovery. As she dug beneath a hedgerow, she noticed something unusual protruding from the soil. On closer inspection she was horrified to find that it was part of a human arm. She hurried to summon the police and soon the bodies of a man and a woman were discovered buried in the shallow grave.

That this was a recent burial was borne out by the fact that one of the bodies was still oozing blood from a wound to the head. The dead pair were identified as Thomas and Emily Kirby, a retired couple from Stockton, and a post-mortem revealed that they had suffered a gruesome death. The old man had been battered about the head and his wife strangled, but both were still alive when they had been put into the ground. Traces of soil were discovered in the mouths of both victims; they had been buried alive and the cause of death in each case was asphyxia.

Police soon had a suspect. Enquiries suggested that one of Emily's grandsons, Charles Conlin, needed to be investigated further. In the weeks before the murders, they learned that Conlin had been short of money, his wages barely covering his rent and food. Yet on the day the bodies were discovered, it was shown that he had purchased a motorcycle in Darlington, costing £21 10s, which he had paid in cash, giving his name as Charles Murphy.

On the evening that the bodies were unearthed, it was found that he had taken his girlfriend out and shown her a quantity of bank notes. Police also learned that on Friday 21 September, Conlin had been at his home at Centenary Crescent, Norton, where he had helped his brother-in-law dig up the garden. Later that evening, he had been out drinking

Durham,

19th November, 1928.

Dear Sir,

2948 Charles William Conlin.
Sentence of Death.

I have to inform you that you have been selected as assistant executioner in the above case. If the prisoner appeals against his conviction or the sentence is respited you will at once be informed.

The date of carrying out the sentence has been provisionally fixed for Tuesday, 4th December, 1928, at 8 a.m.

I enclose a copy of the "Memorandum of Conditions" to which you will be required to conform.

Please inform me by return of post if you accept the service.

Yours faithfully,

Governor.

Mr Frank Rowe, M.M.,
1/241, King Edwards Road,
Ladywood,
Birmingham.

Conlin was due to hang on 4 December and the executioners were engaged for this date. His subsequent appeal postponed the date by one month and he was hanged on 4 January 1929. Frank Rowe tendered his resignation a few days after Conlin was hanged. (Author's collection)

with a friend. They parted before 10 p.m. and when Conlin returned home around midnight, he was driving an Austin 7. A car similar to one Conlin was known to have been driving had been stolen from a house a few minutes away from his home. On the following morning, another lodger at Centenary Crescent saw Conlin carrying a spade as he walked across fields at the back of his house, close to where the bodies were discovered.

Detectives now believed that they had their man. Desperate for money, Conlin knew that Kirby often carried large amounts of cash on him. When police arrested Conlin, they

Illustrated Police News *showing the arrest of Charlie Conlin.* (T.J. Leech archive)

found in his possession a grey wallet identified as belonging to Kirby. Questioned, Conlin claimed he remembered nothing of his movements on the night in question.

He was to stick to this story throughout his trial before Mr Justice Roche at Durham in November 1928. It was suggested to the court that after stealing the car, Conlin had driven 4 miles to his grandparents' home, where he told them a story to get them to leave the house. He then attacked them both, stole from them and concealed their still-conscious bodies in the shallow grave, where they were discovered on the following morning.

49

A MAN TO AVOID

❖ *James Johnson, 7 August 1929* ❖

The Northumberland police were well aware of Jimmy Johnson. The 43-year-old crippled bookmaker of Cannon Street, Newcastle, had a string of gambling and drunk and disorderly convictions dating back over twenty years, and was also known as a violent man who habitually carried a razor. He was also someone known to most of the neighbours as a man to avoid.

On 27 December 1928, he started a sixty-day prison sentence after being convicted of theft in Aberdeen. While he was inside, another bookmaker, Billy Ridley, began to lodge at Cannon Street. When Johnson learned of this arrangement, he suspected that his wife, Mary Ann, and Ridley were having an affair. She strongly denied his accusations but, on his return home after release from gaol, two of her own children told their father that they suspected there was indeed an affair going on. Johnson became enraged and made threats to kill his wife and children. He also threatened Ridley, who strenuously denied the affair and wrote to Johnson challenging him to bring his razors, knives and any friends he wanted to, and to fight him.

On 9 May 1929, Mrs Johnson made a complaint to a PC Urwin about the way her husband was treating her. The officer accompanied her back to the house and spoke to Johnson, warning him of his behaviour. Johnson informed the officer that his wife had assaulted him with a rolling pin. They exchanged further words and finally she reached into her husband's coat, which was hanging on the back of a chair, and withdrew a razor from the pocket. Showing it to the officer, she said, 'This is what he keeps for me.'

At 1 a.m. on the morning of 12 May, a neighbour heard sounds coming from Johnson's house. The noises were so unusual that he roused another neighbour and together they went to investigate. They knocked at Johnson's door but received no answer. There was, however, a strong smell of gas. Forcing the door, they located the gas tap, which had been turned on. They shut off the gas, and as another neighbour hurried to fetch the police, they opened the bedroom and recoiled in horror.

Mary Johnson was lying dead on the bed, her throat cut. In another room, Johnson lay on his bed, his hands heavily bloodstained and barely conscious from inhaling gas fumes. The three children in the house were all affected by gas but each later made a full recovery.

Johnson was charged with the murder of his wife and the attempted murder of his three children. He tried to pass the blame on to his wife, saying that she had committed suicide by cutting her own throat after switching the gas on. His bloodstained hands told a different story and it was enough to convict him. Sentenced to death by Mr Justice Finlay on 3 July, he vigorously protested his innocence in the condemned cell.

50
THE FAMILY FEUD

❖ *Ernest Wadge Parker, 6 December 1933* ❖

Ernie Parker and his twin brother, Sydney, ran a small family greengrocery business and lived, along with the rest of the family, above the shop in Blooms Avenue, West Stanley, County Durham. It was not a happy business and there was often trouble, with Ernie believing that his father, Thomas, and their sister, Lily, were always finding fault with him.

Ernie claimed that his father owed him £20, which the older man denied, and relations became so strained that on 14 December 1932, Parker was bound over for two separate assaults on his father and sister.

On 13 April 1933, he struck Lily again and for this he received a sentence of two months' hard labour. He was released on 17 June and told a neighbour, 'If they start their impudence up again, I will do them both in.' On his return home, his conduct was such that the police had to be called to escort him away. As he was led down the street, he swore, 'I will swing for the buggers yet – I will cut her bloody head off!'

On Sunday 25 June, Parker called at the house and was seen by his niece, 12-year-old Elsie Parker, attacking his sister with an axe. Running into the street, he shouted to a neighbour that he had 'fettled her this time!' The niece rushed to find a policeman and Parker gave himself up without a struggle. Lily Parker was rushed to Newcastle Infirmary, where she died from serious head injuries in the early hours. Placed under arrest, Parker told the officer, 'I hope she is dead, I want the rope.'

At his trial at Durham Assizes on 14 November before Mr Justice Humphreys, his defence was inherited insanity. His mother was declared insane before the birth of Parker and his twin brother. In 1912, she was admitted to Winterton County Mental Hospital, Durham and died there two years later. Both Parker and the sister he had killed had also been inmates at the asylum, in Parker's case for six months from August 1916.

Despite the evidence of insanity, the prosecution put forward a strong case of wilful murder caused through a grievance he had against his sister. Passing sentence, the judge said that he concurred with the verdict. There was no recommendation for mercy and no appeal. Despite the brutal nature of the crime, over 20,000 people signed a petition for a reprieve. A medical panel found that Parker was an unstable and bad-tempered man, but he was sound of mind and there was no reason to interfere with the verdict on medical grounds.

51

THAT CONFOUNDED MONEY

❖ John Stephenson Bainbridge, 9 May 1935 ❖

It was 31 December 1934 and celebrations to welcome in the New Year were well under way. At shortly before 10 p.m., Jane Herdman finished her late-night shopping and caught the omnibus home to see in the New Year with her aged father, 75-year-old solicitor's clerk and well-known local historian Edward Frederick Herdman.

Returning to their home in Salisbury Place, Bishop Auckland, she was surprised to find the door locked and, fearing that her father might have had a seizure or fall, she managed to gain entry through an open window at the back of the house. Her worst fears were confirmed, but in a far more horrifying way than she had imagined.

Salisbury Place, Bishop Auckland, 1935. (Author's collection)

The scene of the crime. (TNA: PRO)

Lying on the dining room floor was the body of her father. However, it was clear that he had not collapsed, but been severely beaten and his throat cut. Beside the body lay a bloodstained silver penknife, and close by was a heavy brass poker covered in blood. Her cries alerted neighbours, one of whom called the police.

Superintendent Headen and Sergeant Middlewood arrived and began a murder investigation. They soon found that a number of things did not add up. Drawers upstairs had been ransacked and the daughter confirmed that money was missing from the house – yet the dead man's bloodstained wallet, which the killer had presumably removed from his pocket, was found on the dining table. It contained £40. In his trouser pocket, police found another large wad of pound notes. It seemed that robbery was the motive but, if so, why had the killer not taken the money from the wallet and the man's pocket? Had he taken just enough for his needs?

The detectives considered the killer's method of entry. Jane Herdman confirmed that all the doors were locked and so it seemed clear that the old man must had invited his murderer into his house. This, they reasoned, meant that he was someone well known to the victim, and they quickly had a prime suspect: John Bainbridge, a 26-year-old neighbour who had been at the house earlier in the evening. He was a soldier home on leave and had been a regular visitor to the house, a few doors down from his mother's, since returning to Bishop Auckland. Jane Herdman told the police that she thought he was short of money. Within hours, Bainbridge was arrested at a party in Gateshead. He denied any involvement in the crime, but when bloodstains were found on his shirt cuff he was arrested on suspicion and held in custody.

Bainbridge was a private in the 1st Battalion Durham Light Infantry, stationed at Blackdown Camp in Hampshire. Before enlisting, he had worked as a junior clerk at the same firm of solicitors where Herdman worked as a managing clerk. Their families were neighbours and well known to each other and, although they lived on the same street, it was in very different circumstances: Herdman lived a comfortable existence, while Bainbridge had been brought up by his widowed mother in much humbler surroundings.

During one of the visits, Bainbridge mentioned that he might be due a posting to the Saar, and the old man suggested that he make a will. Bainbridge agreed that it was a

Illustrated Police News *showing the execution of John Bainbridge*. (T.J. Leech archive)

good idea and on 31 December he purchased a will from a stationer's. That afternoon, Bainbridge called and asked Herdman to draft the will. Later that evening, he called again to see how things were progressing, and when Jane Herdman left the house at 10 minutes to 8, Bainbridge accompanied her and they walked towards her bus stop.

Pathologist Dr McCulloch had determined that the time of death was somewhere between eight and ten o'clock and detectives questioned Bainbridge over his movements during this time. He told them that he had returned home after leaving Herdman's house and his mother confirmed this, adding that while they were talking she heard the clock strike eight o'clock. After a wash and brush up, Bainbridge left, telling his mother he was going to meet his fiancée, Helen Wright, and that they were going to a party in Gateshead. She said that he had been short of money and she had given him half a crown earlier that day.

Investigations found that Bainbridge had called at a jeweller's shop, at about 20 past 8, where he paid the last instalment on an engagement ring and bought some jewellery. He then caught a bus for Gateshead, where he attended the party.

Detectives learned that Bainbridge had been short of money before Christmas. He had borrowed £18 from a moneylender and had failed in a request to obtain more from the same lender. When arrested, he had £5 in his wallet. Asked how he had obtained it,

Bainbridge claimed that he had borrowed the money from a married woman friend but refused to name her.

On 3 January 1935, Private McNally, a soldier at Blackdown Camp, received an envelope postmarked Gateshead, 1 January 1935. It contained thirty-five £1 notes and two 10*s* notes, a number of which were bloodstained. There was no letter inside but the writing on the envelope was similar to that of Bainbridge's found on the draft of his will at the dead man's house.

The police were satisfied that Bainbridge was the killer and he was charged with murder, standing trial at Durham Assizes before Mr Justice Goddard in March. He pleaded not guilty. The evidence against him was in the main circumstantial. He was short of money before the murder, yet shortly after it he had money in his possession, which he spent at the jeweller's, money he still claimed was a loan from a woman whose identity he refused to reveal. He was known to have bought a drink in a Gateshead hotel, paid for with a £1 note which was one of a sequence that matched those sent to the comrade of Bainbridge's at the army camp. Bloodstains on the note were the same as that of the victim and the same group as the stains on Bainbridge's shirt cuff.

His defence was that he had been seen to leave the house by the victim's daughter, and that after visiting his mother he caught an omnibus to Gateshead, where he spent the night in the company of his fiancée. She testified that she did not see any trace of blood on his clothes. The prosecution claimed that there was a ten-minute window in Bainbridge's alibi from leaving the house to speaking with his mother and that this was ample time in which to return to the house, commit the murder and steal the money he needed to settle his debts and pay the final instalment on the engagement ring, with a little extra to pay for drinks in Gateshead. 'There is no alibi for those ten minutes,' the court was told.

After a trial lasting four days, the jury took only a short time to reach their verdict. Passing sentence, Mr Justice Goddard said that after a patient trial the jury had found the prisoner guilty of the murder of an old man whom he had murdered for the sake of his money. There was no recommendation to mercy.

As her son awaited his fate at Durham Gaol, Bainbridge's mother received a letter from a woman who signed herself 'A Great Friend'. She claimed that she was the married woman who had lent him the money, and that Bainbridge was innocent of the murder. 'I cannot come forward as I am in a pretty high position and my husband would do something terrible to the children and myself.'

Following the dismissal of his appeal, Bainbridge wrote to his solicitor, 'Not once did I dream that the result could be as disastrous as this through my refusing to implicate the lady from whom I borrowed that confounded money.'

52
THE BONFIRE PARTY

❖ George Hague, 16 July 1935 ❖

On the night of Monday 6 May 1935, the Fever Hospital at Langley Park, County Durham was holding a bonfire party to celebrate King George V's silver jubilee. Twenty-year-old Amanda Sharp worked at the hospital and had been courting George Hague, a 23-year-old unemployed bus driver, since Christmas 1934. On the previous afternoon, they had been out for a drink with friends when he mentioned the bonfire. George assumed that he would be accompanying Amanda to the party, but she told him that the matron had forbidden the nurses to go with their young men. Her friend also worked at the hospital and questioned this statement. She was going with her boyfriend and was not aware of any ruling forbidding partners. Amanda was adamant that she did not intend going to the bonfire with George, repeating what the matron had said.

George sensed that something was wrong and asked Amanda to return a brightly coloured handkerchief he had given her as a love token. On the Monday evening George went to the hospital and saw Amanda at the bonfire with a number of workmates. Other nurses and staff were at the fire, many in the company of boyfriends and husbands. Amanda handed back the handkerchief to Hague and left the bonfire early, as she had to return home and change to be ready for the night shift.

She was due back on duty at 11.30 p.m. and as she walked up the driveway with a colleague, she found Hague waiting. He asked to speak to Amanda, who, agreeing to his request, told her friend to go on ahead. Moments later, her friend heard a

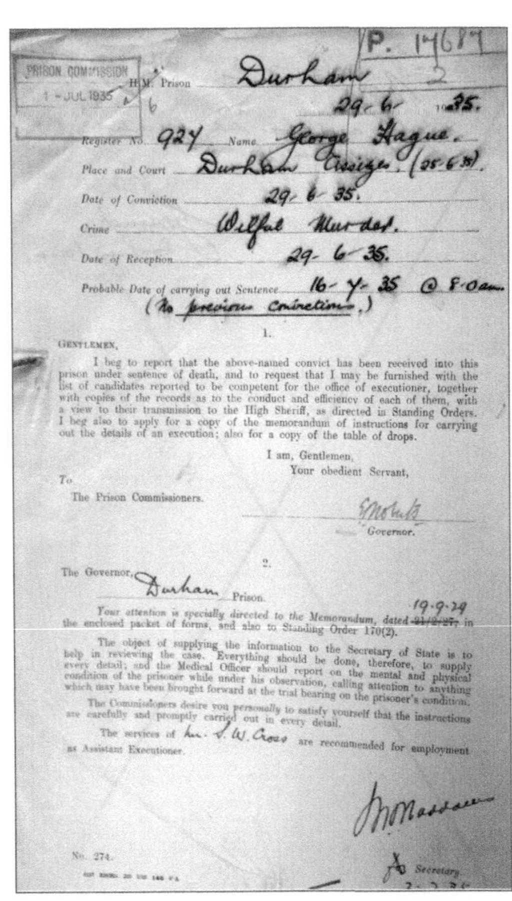

P. 14687

PRISON COMMISSION 1 - JUL 1935

H.M. Prison Durham

29-6- 1935.

Register No. 924 Name George Hague.

Place and Court Durham Assizes. (25-6-35).

Date of Conviction 29-6-35.

Crime Wilful Murder.

Date of Reception 29-6-35.

Probable Date of carrying out Sentence 16-7-35 @ 8.0 a.m.

(No previous convictions.)

1.

GENTLEMEN,

I beg to report that the above-named convict has been received into this prison under sentence of death, and to request that I may be furnished with the list of candidates reported to be competent for the office of executioner, together with copies of the records as to the conduct and efficiency of each of them, with a view to their transmission to the High Sheriff, as directed in Standing Orders. I beg also to apply for a copy of the memorandum of instructions for carrying out the details of an execution; also for a copy of the table of drops.

I am, Gentlemen,
Your obedient Servant,

To
The Prison Commissioners.

Governor.

2.

The Governor,
Durham Prison.

Your attention is specially directed to the Memorandum, dated ~~21/2/27,~~ 19.9.29 in the enclosed packet of forms, and also to Standing Order 170(2).

The object of supplying the information to the Secretary of State is to help in reviewing the case. Everything should be done, therefore, to supply every detail; and the Medical Officer should report on the mental and physical condition of the prisoner while under his observation, calling attention to anything which may have been brought forward at the trial bearing on the prisoner's condition.

The Commissioners desire you *personally* to satisfy yourself that the instructions are carefully and promptly carried out in every detail.

The services of Mr. T. W. Cross are recommended for employment as Assistant Executioner.

Secretary.

No. 274.

Official confirmation of sentence of death passed on George Hague. (Crime Picture Archive)

Chronicle

"WORLD"

7, 1935 PRICE ONE PENNY

The New Low Prices For BEAVAN'S FAMOUS "TWO-X" RANGE

NO PLACE LIKE BEAVAN'S FOR CARPETS

Shields Road, Newcastle-on-Tyne.

JUBILEE CELEBRATIONS

LANGLEY BUSMAN ON MURDER CHARGE

HOSPITAL MAID'S DEATH ON ROAD SEQUEL

ACCUSED REMANDED

THE discovery of a girl's body on the road to the Langley Park Isolation Hospital shortly after midnight had a sequel at Consett Police Court to-day when an unemployed bus conductor named George Hague of Langley Park, was charged with murder, and was remanded for eight days.

PLEA TO SEE SISTER

the crowd, from the State Coach, during yesterday's sion through London.

THE ACCUSED, George Hague (23), ... the witness box, and after a short ...

Hague's murder made the headlines on the day of the King's Jubilee. (T.J. Leech collection)

scream and turned to see Amanda lying on the ground. Hague stood over her with a razor in his hand. As he fled the scene, Amanda was assisted to the hospital and given medical attention, but she was suffering from a severe throat wound and died within a few minutes.

Hague was arrested at his home in the early hours. At his trial at Durham Assizes on Sunday 30 June, the prosecution claimed that it was simply a case of a lover spurned. He took the returning of his love token as a sign that the relationship was over and in a jealous rage he committed a brutal murder.

Hague's defence was a plea of insanity based on a history of mental illness in the family. A cousin was a patient in the Durham County Mental Hospital, an aunt had died in a similar establishment in Yorkshire and his elder brother had committed suicide. However, the defence was unsuccessful, and Mr Justice de Parcq sentenced him to death after a two-day trial.

53

THE PERSISTENT THIEF

❖ *Christopher Jackson, 16 December 1936* ❖

Christopher Jackson had financial problems. Again. And as before, he knew just how to remedy it. Being pressed to pay his rent, the 24-year-old Rotherham-born labourer told his landlady that he was going to Catterick to collect some money he was owed. On the afternoon of 30 June 1936, he left his lodgings at Chester-le-Street, and when he returned later that night he paid £2 for his lodgings and settled a number of debts with his landlady and fellow tenants.

On the following morning, police called at the Chester-le-Street lodging house and questioned Jackson about his movements on the previous day. Jackson asked why they wanted to know and was told that they were investigating the brutal murder of his aunt at Sunderland. Jackson was an immediate suspect: he had a long criminal record for theft, he had served a sentence in Borstal for stealing from a relative, and in the previous year he had been dismissed from the army for theft.

Christopher Jackson. (Author's collection)

Late on the previous afternoon, a neighbour had spotted a tall stranger outside the house of Mrs Harriet May Linney, a 61-year-old bookmaker. Harriet and her husband Thomas had both retired but still ran the small bookmaking business from home. Thomas had left the house that morning to go to Carlisle races, where he worked as a trackside bookie. At 8 p.m. another neighbour noticed the back door open and, going to investigate, discovered the body of Mrs Linney lying on the kitchen floor. She had been battered to death with a bottle and heavy coal rake.

Taken in for further questioning, Jackson told police he had been in Catterick, but when a search of his room found almost £10 in silver concealed in a suitcase, he made a statement admitting that he had lied. He said that he had travelled to Sunderland to see his aunt and uncle to ask for a loan. Earlier that summer, he had asked for a loan and they had given him a small sum.

Jackson stated that he called at the house and found that his uncle was away at Carlisle races. His aunt let him wait in the house until his uncle returned and offered him a drink. He said she began to insult and push him, berating him for continuing to ask for money and not being able to hold down a regular job. Jackson claimed he lost his temper, punched her in the face and then hit her first with a coal rake, before battering her about the head with the beer bottle.

Jackson's counsel pleaded for a verdict of manslaughter on the grounds of provocation when he stood trial at Durham Assizes before Mr Justice Goddard on 4 November. The story now was that his aunt had attacked him first with a flat iron and he had only hit back in retaliation. He claimed to have had no intention of killing her but medical evidence found that she had been struck four times on top of her head and twice in the face. This suggested more than simple retaliation and, rejecting the manslaughter plea, the jury found him guilty of murder.

54

CIRCUMSTANTIAL EVIDENCE

❖ *Robert William Hoolhouse, 26 May 1938* ❖

On the afternoon of Tuesday 18 January 1938, 67-year-old farmer's wife Mrs Margaret Jane Dobson left her home at High Grange Farm, Wolviston, County Durham. When she failed to return home that night, her husband assumed that she was staying overnight at their daughter's home in Newcastle. On the following morning, as he left the farm to walk into the village of Wolviston, he discovered the body of his wife in a field close to the farm. She had been brutally raped and stabbed to death.

After questioning all the young men in the village, police soon had a prime suspect and a possible motive, and in the early hours of 20 January, Robert Hoolhouse, a 21-year-old farm labourer of Pickering Street, Haverton Hill, was taken into custody. Detectives learned that in 1933 the Hoolhouse family had worked for Mr Dobson until they had an argument, when the family lost their jobs and were evicted from the tied cottage they rented.

Hoolhouse had scratches on his face and traces of blood were found on his clothing. Asked to account for his movements on the day of the murder, he gave police a detailed statement. He claimed that on the afternoon of 18 January, he had been at home until noon, then had cycled to Wolviston to the home of William Husband. He stayed there

Detectives stand beside the body of Mrs Dobson on the path to High Grange Farm. (Author's collection)

until 3.30 p.m., when he left to cycle home via Cowpen. The journey took thirty minutes. At 6.30 p.m., he caught the bus to Wolviston, where he again visited Husband and where he met up with Dolly Lax. Hoolhouse and Dolly caught a bus to Billingham, where they went to the cinema. At 11 p.m., after seeing Dolly on to the bus for Wolviston, he caught his own bus, for Haverton, and arrived home thirty minutes later.

On the following morning, he said he was at home until he left to visit the Labour Exchange at 10.45 a.m. After taking a walk, he returned home for lunch, before cycling to Wolviston, where he fell off his bicycle and scratched his face.

Checking what seemed a detailed alibi, detectives soon found a discrepancy. Police were told that Hoolhouse had left Husband's house an hour later than he had originally stated, and thus he was not home at 5 p.m., as he had claimed. Hoolhouse then made a second statement, in which he admitted that he must have got the times wrong.

This was of great significance. A pathologist told detectives that an examination of Mrs Dobson's stomach contents put the time of death after 4 p.m., and he believed it to have been around 5 p.m. This suggested that Hoolhouse had deliberately lied to give himself an alibi for the time of the murder.

At his three-day trial, before Mr Justice Wrottersley at Leeds Assizes beginning on 30 March, the prosecution portrayed Hoolhouse as a callous killer who had taken a girlfriend

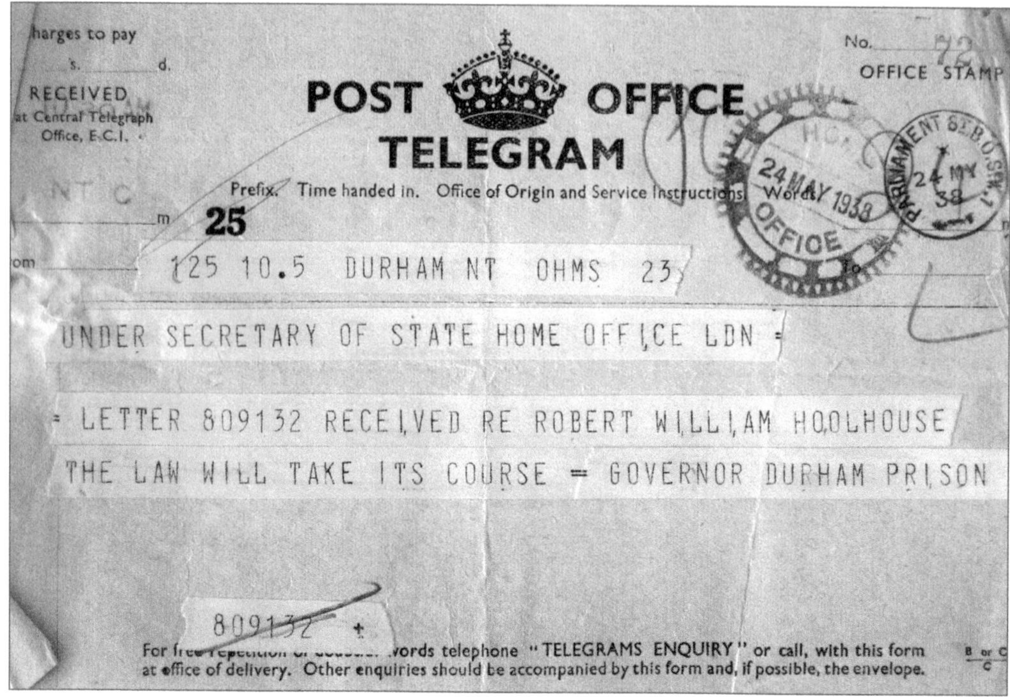

harges to pay s. d.
RECEIVED at Central Telegraph Office, E.C.I.

POST OFFICE TELEGRAM

No.

OFFICE STAMP

Prefix. Time handed in. Office of Origin and Service Instructions. Words.

25

125 10.5 DURHAM NT OHMS 23

UNDER SECRETARY OF STATE HOME OFFICE LDN

= LETTER 809132 RECEIVED RE ROBERT WILLIAM HOOLHOUSE THE LAW WILL TAKE ITS COURSE = GOVERNOR DURHAM PRISON

809132 +

For f[illegible] words telephone "TELEGRAMS ENQUIRY" or call, with this form at office of delivery. Other enquiries should be accompanied by this form and, if possible, the envelope.

Telegram from the Home Office informing the governor at Durham that 'the law will take its course'. (Crime Picture Archive)

to the cinema hours after committing a brutal crime. Although there was no direct evidence linking Hoolhouse to the murder, there was what the judge deemed 'an accumulation of circumstantial evidence'. He had a possible motive, his description fitted that of a man seen near the farm on the afternoon of the murder, he had scratches on his face, and faint bloodstains found on his clothes matched those of the dead woman. Hoolhouse refused to have a blood test to support his claim that it was his own blood, caused by a burst boil.

Hoolhouse's defence counsel failed to contest the evidence against him fully. A witness at the farm testified that he had seen a man near the farm at 5.30 p.m. and he swore it was not Hoolhouse, whom he knew well. If this man was the killer, it could not be the accused, as he was known to have been at home at that time.

The evidence of the scratches on Hoolhouse's face was also not properly explained. Mrs Dobson was wearing heavy woollen gloves when she was killed. Police experiments failed to replicate the scratches found on Hoolhouse's face using these gloves, and a footprint found next to the body did not match that of Hoolhouse. One other telling clue that could have proved the innocence of Hoolhouse was the lack of semen stains on his clothing. When arrested, he was wearing the same clothes he had worn on the previous day, and although Mrs Dobson had been raped and there were extensive semen stains on her body, there was no trace on his clothes. The defence also provided medical reports showing that he had a mental age of less than 14, but it was to no avail.

The jury took over four hours to consider their verdict before finding Hoolhouse guilty as charged. There were cries of disbelief as the verdict was returned and many in the gallery were in tears as sentence of death was passed. So convinced were his parents that he would be acquitted that they even had a taxi waiting to take them home. Hoolhouse's appeal failed on 9 May. The three appeal judges concurred with the original verdict, believing the prosecution's view that he had gone to the farm, where he had happened upon Mrs Dobson. As there was still ill feeling between them, she had ordered him off the property, whereupon he had attacked and killed her.

A petition of 14,000 signatures failed to sway the Home Secretary, and Hoolhouse was executed on a foggy May morning. He had been a keen pigeon fancier, and as he waited in the condemned cell it was reported that his favourite bird was often seen sitting on the prison wall. On the morning of his execution, the bird was again seen sitting on the wall. As the bell began to toll the fateful hour, the bird flew away. It was never seen again.

55

SUICIDE OR MURDER?

❖ *William Parker, 26 July 1938* ❖

William and Jane Parker had married in 1936. By the spring of 1938, they were living in a flat at Edwin's Avenue, Forest Hall and had two children, a 1-year-old girl, Shirley, and a baby boy, Cecil, just a few months old. Parker, aged 25, had worked as a miner but, unable to hold down regular work, he now earned a living as a golf caddie at Benton and Gosforth Park golf courses.

On 25 April 1938, Parker walked into Forest Hall police station and told officers that he was responsible for the death of his wife, three days before. He told them that there were two other bodies in his house. Jane Parker had been battered and a length of string was knotted tightly around her neck. A pathologist confirmed the cause of death as strangulation, before she was struck nine times with a hammer. The two children had also been strangled, and both had string knotted around their necks.

Parker told police that he had arrived home to find his wife had strangled their two children and then attacked him with a hammer. He had then killed his wife in self-defence, battering her with the hammer. He said that afterwards he had caddied as normal and had slept at his mother's house.

Tried before Mr Justice Atkinson at Newcastle Assizes on 17 June, Parker claimed responsibility for only the death of his wife. His story was that he had returned home

FOREST HALL MAN EXECUTED FOR WIFE MURDER

Small Crowd Waits Outside Prison

WILLIAM PARKER, the 25-year-old golf caddie and miner, of Forest Hall, was executed in Durham Prison at 8 a.m. to-day for the murder of his wife, Jane, in their flat at Edwin's Avenue, Forest Hall, on April 22.

The executioner was Pierrepoint. Not more than 20 people, including several women, waited outside the prison. As the Cathedral clock chimed the hour the men bared their heads.

Seven minutes later the official notice that the execution had been duly carried out was posted at the gates by a warder.

Among the small number of persons congregated outside the prison were police officers who were on duty at the entrance to the Assize Courts and prison grounds.

SECOND HANGING

The "Evening Chronicle" was informed by a prison official, who was present, that

News cutting reporting Parker's execution. (T.J. Leech collection)

to find his wife with her hands around the throat of their son. Parker claimed that his wife had strangled both the children and she then rushed at him with a poker. She chased him into the scullery, where he picked up a hammer and battered her about the head. He then said that, in revenge for what she had done to the children, he took some string and tightly knotted it around her neck.

The defence also claimed that, shortly before she died, Mrs Parker told a neighbour she was in despair at their financial situation, not helped by her husband's gambling, and that she planned to commit suicide and kill the children too.

The prosecution claimed that there was no evidence that his wife had killed the children, and although Parker never wavered from his story, the court found him guilty. He fainted when sentence of death was passed on him and cried out, 'Oh, Jane, why did you do it?' Charges for the murder of the children were not taken any further.

56

THE FULL MOON KILLER

❖ *John Daymond, 8 February 1939* ❖

Money was the root of all John Daymond's problems. On 7 November 1938, the 19-year-old farm hand failed to turn up for work at William Foster's farm, and as a result he was dismissed the following day. This hit Daymond hard; he already owed money to several people and a firm of solicitors was pursuing one of the debts.

Daymond burst into tears when he was told that he was too unreliable to keep his job, and although he was owed no wages, Foster gave him a shilling out of kindness. On the following day Daymond bumped into James Percival, the son of another former employer. Daymond had done some casual work haymaking that summer and knew that the Percivals were well off. Again Daymond pleaded poverty, telling him that he not eaten that day and he only had a halfpenny to his name.

TIMES, SATURDAY, JANUARY 21, 1939.

Murder—Two Days After Full Moon

"Strange Coincidence" In Wigton Crime

Death Sentence On Young Farm Hand

SENTENCE of death was passed by Mr. Justice Croom-Johnson on John Daymond, a nineteen-years-old farm labourer, of no fixed address, at the Cumberland Assizes at Carlisle on Wednesday, when he was found guilty of murdering James Irwin Percival, senior, his former employer, at

help them as to accused's condition at the material time. Accused was just about the age at which he would be most liable to an attack of schizophrenia, and, as they had heard, this disease might come after a period of great physical or mental stress. Accused had not had food for two days

Newspaper headline reporting sentence of death passed on Daymond. (Author's collection)

At a few minutes past 7 on the morning of 9 November, Kate Percival was reading a letter in the front room at her farm at Aikhead, near Wigton, Cumbria, when she heard a strange sound coming from outside. Going to investigate, she stumbled on the battered bodies of her father and brother, both named James Percival. Both were taken to Cumberland Infirmary, where the father died from his injuries that afternoon.

With the two men in hospital, police searched the farm, where they discovered John Daymond hiding in a hayloft. He admitted attacking the Percivals with the bloodstained pick found close by. He said he had crept up on the father and battered him with the pick before rummaging through his pockets. The son then appeared and he too was then battered about the head. Daymond's brutal attack had yielded him less than 3s.

Daymond's defence when he stood trial at Cumberland Assizes at Carlisle was insanity. His counsel blamed the full moon that was in the sky on the night prior to the murder for rendering his client insane. Witnesses were called to show traces of insanity in the family, but, as the prosecution pointed out, it was a brutal crime committed in the furtherance of theft. The father had been struck five blows, and when Daymond was spotted, he struck the son in order to get away.

Daymond was duly sentenced to death, although the jury added a strong recommendation to mercy on account of his youth. There was no appeal and, reviewing the case, the Home Secretary decided that age alone was not justification for a reprieve and saw no reason to interfere with the due process of law.

57

LET HIM HAVE IT!

❖ William Appleby and Vincent Ostler, 11 July 1940 ❖

William Appleby. (T.J. Leech collection)

It was a miner making his way home down Westley Road, Coxhoe, County Durham in the early hours of Thursday 29 February 1940 who alerted the police. Passing the Co-operative store, Jeff Smith noticed a light flicker in the top-floor window. In the blackout that was in force throughout the country, it was enough to draw attention; in a grocery store closed for the day, it was enough to raise suspicion. Just as quickly as it appeared, it was extinguished. But Smith had caught sight of a face at the window and, assuming a robbery was taking place, he hurried to the local police station.

Police Constable William Shiell and war reserve constable William Stafford were on duty and, accompanied by Smith and another miner who was chatting to the bobbies, they hurried to the store. Shiell shone his torch through the front window but all seemed quiet. Making their way round the back, they found that the bolts had been removed from the door. Shiell returned to the front, leaving his colleague to guard the back door.

Shiell shone his torch inside and this time the large front window crashed open and two men made their getaway. Hearing the glass breaking and the urgent blasts coming from Shiell's police whistle, Stafford and Smith raced round to the front and saw Constable Shiell in hot pursuit of two men. The men had reached the end of the street in the direction of waste ground near Long Row, when a shot rang out. Seconds later a car revved up and screeched away.

William Shiell was found lying in the dirt, a bullet wound in his stomach. An ambulance raced him to hospital and, as colleagues and friends rushed to the hospital offering to give blood in the hope it would help the stricken constable, Shiell was told that his injuries were so severe that he was going to die. He made a dying declaration in which he said that there were two men, one of whom was armed, and the unarmed man had shouted to his accomplice, 'Let him have it.' At 4.30 on the morning of 1 March, Police Constable William Ralph Shiell died from his injuries. He was just 28 years old and left a wife and 3-year-old daughter.

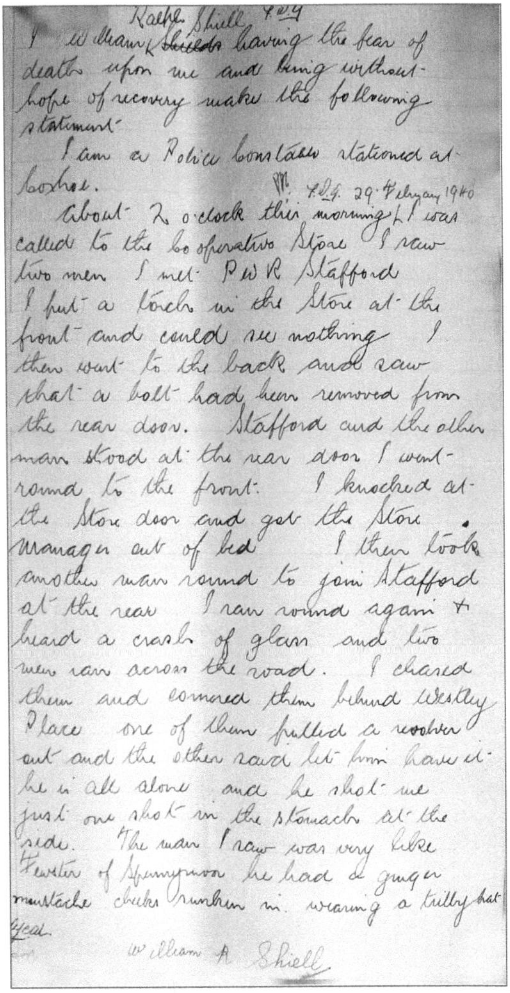
Ralph Shiell 429
I William Shields having the fear of death upon me and being without hope of recovery make the following statement.
I am a Police Constable stationed at Coxhoe.
429. 29 February 1940
About 2 o'clock this morning I was called to the Co-operative Store I saw two men I met PWR Stafford
I put a torch in the Store at the front and could see nothing I then went to the back and saw that a bolt had been removed from the rear door. Stafford and the other man stood at the rear door I went round to the front. I knocked at the Store door and got the Store manager out of bed I then took another man round to join Stafford at the rear I ran round again & heard a crash of glass and two men ran across the road. I chased them and cornered them behind Westley Place one of them pulled a revolver out and the other said let him have it. he is all alone and he shot me just one shot in the stomach at the side. The man I saw was very like Fewster of Spennymoor he had a ginger moustache cheeks sunken in wearing a trilby hat
year
William A Shiell

PC Shiell's deathbed statement. (TNA: PRO)

Durham Constabulary offered a reward of £100 for information, but police already had a number of clues to work on. A toolbox had been found in the shop and tracks made by the getaway car were thought to belong to a grey Vauxhall similar to one stolen from a doctor in Chester-le-Street a week earlier. Witnesses came forward to say that two petty crooks were driving a similar car shortly before the shooting.

In the early hours of 4 March, 24-year-old Vincent Ostler and 27-year-old William Appleby, two petty thieves, were picked up by the police at Hawksworth, near Bradford. Under questioning, Appleby, a joiner who made coffins, admitted that they had gone to rob the store, but it had been Ostler who fired the fatal shot. He said he did not know that Ostler was carrying a gun, and strenuously denied encouraging the shooting with the words: 'Let him have it.'

Vincent Ostler. (T.J. Leech collection)

Ostler, an ice-cream man and the son of a former police sergeant, claimed that he was at home at the time of the murder, and his father, dismissed from the force, backed his son up. Ostler was then told that Appleby had confessed and was taken into custody. As the two were escorted to Durham Gaol to await their trial, wardens overheard Ostler tell his erstwhile friend, 'If you had kept your mouth shut, they wouldn't have a case against us and we would have been in the clear.'

They were tried before Mr Justice Hilbery at Leeds Assizes in May. Appleby denied PC Shiell's deathbed claim that he had shouted, 'Let him have it!' instead insisting that he told Ostler to 'give him a clout!' However, the declaration of a dying policeman was never questioned. Although it was never in doubt that Ostler had fired the fatal shot, Appleby was judged to have encouraged him and was therefore equally guilty. On 10 May, after a four-day trial, both were sentenced to death, with the jury according Appleby a strong recommendation for mercy.

Twelve years later, the very same words and claims were heard in the Craig and Bentley case, when a policeman was shot in south London. Nineteen-year-old Derek Bentley, who was hanged alone, as his accomplice Craig was only 16 and hence too young to be executed, claimed never to have encouraged his friend to 'Let him have it'. Coincidence? Or did this case have a far more sinister impact on the London teenager?

58

TELLTALE SPECKS OF BLOOD

❖ *John Wright, 10 September 1940* ❖

Schoolchildren returning home for lunch made the horrific discovery. It was 12.20 p.m. on Wednesday 22 May 1940 and, entering the kitchen at their home at Pixley Hills, near Bishop Auckland, they discovered their mother Alice Wright lying severely battered on the kitchen floor.

DEATH SENTENCE

Toronto Man to Pay the Penalty

"I am innocent. I did not kill my wife." So declared John William Wright, aged 41, an unemployed brickyard labourer, of Pixley Hills, Toronto, Bishop Auckland, after a jury at Leeds Assizes on Thursday had found him "guilty" of the wilful murder of his 43-year-old wife, Alice, on May 22nd. He was sentenced to death by Mr Justice Stable.

The case for the prosecution, conducted by Mr C. Paley Scott, K.C., was that the children, on returning from school at midday, found their mother lying on the floor of the cottage with her head battered in. Wright told the police that she was all right when he left the house at 10 o'clock that morning. A butcher's cleaver, bearing traces of human blood, was found in a cupboard, and there were spots of blood on Wright's shirt, although he had no cut or scratch himself.

BLOOD ON SHIRT

The blood on the shirt, the prosecution alleged, was of the same group as Mrs Wright's. Asked by the police to explain its presence, Wright said he might have got it when he put a coat over his wife after the discovery. The prosecution pointed out that at that time his shirt was covered by a waistcoat and muffler.

Wright and his wife, it was alleged, had quarrelled the previous night about an insurance payment she made, partly in respect of a policy on her own life. That morning Wright visited the insurance official, and asked "if the insurances were all right" at a time (the prosecution alleged) when his wife was "lying in her own blood on the floor of the cottage." Wright told the police that it was on his wife's instruction that he called to inquire about the insurance.

When the hearing was resumed on Thursday Wright's counsel, Mr Willard Sexton, submitted that the evidence against him was so slight that the case could properly be withdrawn from the jury. The Judge, however, ruled that there was a prima facie case.

In evidence, Wright said he was married in 1925. He had had quarrels with his wife, but not violent ones. Nine years ago, and again 12 months since, he had had reason to complain of her going about with other men.

On the night before his wife's death he was chopping sticks with the cleaver, which he left against a wall. During the evening they had a few words about 10s she had given to an insurance agent, but the trouble died down.

Next morning, on his wife's instruction, he went to Willington to make inquiries about insurance policies.

Returning at 12.30, he met his next door neighbour, a Mr Gibson, who said Mrs Wright had been found lying in the kitchen in a pool of blood. He directed Gibson to the doctor's and went home. In holding his wife he might have got bloodstains on his clothing.

The execution of Wright has been provisionally fixed for August 6th in Durham Gaol.

Above and below: *Despite the thin wartime newspapers concentrating mainly on events in Europe, the trial and execution of John Wright still made the headlines in the local press*. (Author's collection)

Although unconscious, with blood seeping out of dreadful head wounds, 43-year-old Alice was still alive and, after the children alerted a neighbour, a doctor was sent for and an ambulance summoned. Her husband, John Wright, two years her junior, returned home before the doctor arrived and, seeing his wife on the floor, took off his coat and covered her with it, seeming genuinely upset as he tried to comfort her. Within minutes, the ambulance reached the house and Alice was rushed to the Durham County Hospital, where she died from her injuries without regaining consciousness.

An autopsy found that death was due to severe head injuries: six wounds made by a heavy weapon such as an axe. Police searched the house and, hidden in a cupboard beneath the stairs, they discovered a butcher's cleaver, which appeared to have faint traces of human blood upon it.

This suggested an inside job. Would a stranger go to the trouble of hiding the murder weapon

TORONTO MURDERER EXECUTED

ATTACKED WIFE AFTER QUARREL

Within Durham Gaol on Tuesday, John William Wright, aged 41, an unemployed brickyard worker, was executed for the wilful murder of his 43-year-old wife, Alice, at their home Pixley Hills, Toronto, Bishop Auckland. Pierrepoint was the executioner.

Wright was sentenced to death at Leeds Assizes in July. From the outset he protested his innocence, and after the jury had found him "Guilty" he exclaimed, "I did not kill my wife."

The Court of Criminal Appeal dismissed his appeal against conviction last month and Wright had since occupied the condemned cell in Durham Prison where he was frequently visited by Major A. J. Groom, a Salvation Army Chaplain from Newcastle.

(Author's collection)

inside the house? The police thought not and suspicion immediately fell on the husband. John Wright claimed that he had been using the cleaver to chop wood the previous night and had left it out. He was arrested and charged with murder when routine tests on his clothes found spots of blood of the same type as Alice's on his shirt. Wright claimed that the blood must have got there when he took off his coat to cover his wife while awaiting the ambulance.

This proved to be the crux of the prosecution case when Wright stood before Mr Justice Stable at Leeds Assizes on 25 July. Forensic evidence showed that it was impossible for the blood to have got on Wright's shirt, as a waistcoat had covered the part of the shirt with the bloodstains. These bloodstains, known as 'travelling blood', had seemingly sprayed on to his clothes as he administered the fatal blows.

Throughout his trial, John Wright maintained his innocence. Evidence was heard that Wright and his wife had argued on the night before the murder over payments on an insurance policy, and that on the morning of the murder he had gone to the insurance company offices in nearby Willington to check that his wife's life policy was in place.

The evidence against Wright was mainly circumstantial; there were no witnesses to the attack nor was there any real motive for the crime. He admitted that during their fifteen-year marriage his wife had had several affairs, and the prosecution suggested that this, coupled with the argument over the insurance policy, had turned John Wright into a murderer.

It was a weak motive but the faint bloodstain on Wright's shirt could not adequately be explained and it was enough to convince the jury of his guilt. Wright appealed against the guilty verdict, blaming the judge for misdirecting the jury. But the appeal was quickly dismissed.

59

HANGED ON CHRISTMAS EVE

❖ Edward Scollen, 24 December 1940 ❖

Edward and Beatrice Scollen had been living happily together until a few weeks before the outbreak of the Second World War. For both, it was their second marriage, and they each had three children from their earlier marriage. They lived at a variety of addresses before they settled at St Paul's Road, Middlesbrough. Scollen, a 42-year-old labourer, had already had a few run-ins with his wife's brothers over an inheritance she was due to receive following the death of her first husband, and there was bad feeling and an uneasy peace between him and her family.

In July 1939, a fierce argument broke out over items of furniture that Beatrice had sold to her relatives. The row became so heated that the couple split up and she moved out of their home, only to return a few days later. After a few months another row broke out, this time over 10*s* owed by her brother for the furniture she had sold.

Once again Beatrice moved out, this time for a full week. On 31 July, there was another quarrel, again over money, and again Beatrice walked out. This time she went to stay with friends at North Skelton and did not come back.

On 12 August, Beatrice went to visit her brother, who lived just a few doors away from Scollen. Hearing this, he called at a public house at lunchtime and drank seven pints of beer in two hours. He then went to work, but after clocking on realised he was too drunk and returned home, stopping off for more drink on the way. He decided he would now speak to Beatrice and ask her to return to him.

He found her at a friend's home and they went outside into the back alley, where he asked her to come home with him. She said she would, but only if he agreed that they would find another house. What happened next was debated at his trial before Mr Justice Cassels at York Assizes.

Scollen claimed that he must have blacked out and the last thing he remembered was his wife standing against him, her arms around his neck. He tried to take her home but she fell to the ground. Thinking she had fainted, he returned home to get help. Beatrice Scollen had been stabbed in the back and died shortly afterwards.

Police called at Scollen's house and, finding it locked, broke the door down. They found that he had slashed his wrists and had attempted to hang himself, the rope having embedded itself deeply into his neck. He was cut down and taken to the local infirmary, where, after a stay of five weeks, he was deemed well enough to stand trial.

The prosecution alleged that he had stabbed his wife because she would not return to him. Scollen's defence maintained that he had no knowledge of the crime as he had been too drunk to form the intent. The fact that he had been able to form the intent to commit suicide following her murder showed he was not too incapacitated and, after a trial lasting just over seven hours, one hour of which included the jury debating the verdict, they concluded that, although the defendant may have consumed a large amount of alcohol, he was aware of his actions. He was hanged on Christmas Eve.

60

DOUBLE STANDARDS

❖ *Henry Lyndo White, 6 March 1941* ❖

It was 6.30 p.m. on 19 January 1941, and 17-year-old William Elliott was making his way home down Bertram Street, South Shields, when he saw a man and a woman on the other side of the road. The man, whom he knew as Henry Lyndo White, placed his arms around

March. 6 1941

Henry Lyndo White.

Height. 5 ft 8½ ins

Age 39 years Weight. 156. lbs

Drop 7 ft – 2"

Remarks.

Very quiet culprit, walked without aid and stood correct. The chief executioner was Thomas William Pierrepoint and the job was carried out at H.M. Prison Durham.
Culprit was a married man who cut the throat of a sweetheart.

Assistant hangman Harry Allen recorded the details of Henry Lyndo White's execution in his diary. (Author's collection) her neck, and seeing that the woman appeared to be in some distress Elliott crossed the road to intervene.

As he approached, the woman, whom he also recognised as Emily Wardle, shouted for help. Elliott told White to leave the girl alone. White said it had nothing to do with Elliot, and that Emily would be staying where she was until he had finished with her. White was a much bigger and older man, and Elliott was unwilling to get further involved. Moreover, it could have been just a lovers' tiff. Elliott decided to walk away.

Moments later, he turned round again and saw White put his hand inside his jacket pocket, withdraw a razor and draw it across Emily's throat. As White crossed over the road, Elliott hurried to help and took Emily into a nearby shop. White watched from across the street and called out, 'I told you I'd kill you, Emily you bugger, meeting someone else and double-crossing me.'

As Elliott rushed to fetch the police, White calmly walked over to the shop and sat on the counter. Ernie Unwin, the shopkeeper, told White that Emily was dead, at which he smiled and said there was now going to be another death. He then pulled out the razor and cut his own throat and left wrist, although neither wound was life-threatening. The police arrived and White was rushed to hospital, where, after treatment, he was charged with the murder.

At his trial before Mr Justice Charles at Durham Assizes on St Valentines Day, White's weak defence of provocation failed, the jury being satisfied that there was clear premeditation in a man walking around with a shaving razor on his person. The motive was jealousy. White was a married man with four children. He had been having an affair with Emily for seven years when he developed the suspicion that she was seeing another man.

It was a simple case of double standards. White believed that, while it was acceptable for him to carry on two relationships simultaneously, the same did not hold true for Emily Wardle.

61

SWIFT JUSTICE

❖ *Edward Walker Anderson, 31 July 1941* ❖

William Anderson did not trust banks. During his lifetime, he had amassed a considerable amount of money, preferring to keep it hidden at home rather than in the branch of his local bank. The 63-year-old pensioner was totally blind, but did not let the disability stop him being fit and active. He was fortunate to have his family living close to his home at Moor End, Belmont, Durham.

William shared his home with his nephew, Joseph Anderson. Next door lived William's brother Alfred. The old man also had a housekeeper, Mrs Ethel Carr, who usually arrived at the house at 10 a.m. to start her daily chores.

Moor End, Belmont. (Author's collection)

Joseph Anderson had been lodging with his uncle following his divorce many years before, and worked as a postman. He was an early riser and on 11 June 1941 he was up at first light. He prepared breakfast for his uncle before leaving for work at 10 minutes past 7. At a few minutes to 10, Mrs Carr arrived at the house and was surprised to find the back door locked. She knocked and shouted through the letterbox and, unable to gain entry, she called next door and expressed her concerns to Alfred Anderson.

Alfred did not have a key but, seeing an upstairs window partly open, he used a ladder to gain entry. It was clear that something was amiss: the bedroom had been ransacked. To his horror he found his brother William lying at the bottom of the stairs close to the front door. He appeared to have been severely beaten with a blunt instrument and was covered in blood. William was seriously injured but still alive and as he was rushed to hospital, detectives arrived at Belmont to investigate.

It was quickly established that the old man had been brutally battered with an axe. The life savings that had been hidden upstairs in the house were now missing. Also missing were a fountain pen and a raincoat, which the attacker had probably taken to cover the bloodstains. It seemed clear that whoever had broken into the house knew where to look, as the search had concentrated on the old man's bedroom. For this reason, the immediate suspects were those familiar with the routine of the house, including members of the family.

One name soon stood out. Nineteen-year-old Edward Anderson was the son of Joseph Anderson. He had a criminal record for theft, and just a week earlier he had been released after serving three months' hard labour for theft from the hotel where he had been employed. Following his father's divorce he had spent a lot of time homeless and had done various jobs, including spending some time at sea. His last job had been as a porter at the Grand Hotel, Tynemouth, but that had ended in March when he was convicted of theft.

Superintendent Johnson of the Durham County Constabulary traced Anderson to an address in Hull, where he was lodging. On 13 June, police called at the house and found a number of items that had been stolen from William Anderson's house, including a fountain pen, shoes and a raincoat. Charged with assault, Anderson confessed that he had attacked his uncle and stolen the items.

He told the police that he had slept rough on the night before the attack and had watched to see his father leave for work. He knew that his great uncle kept money in his bedroom and entered the house quietly, hoping to steal the money without being disturbed. He said that, as he crept up the stairs, the old man heard a noise and, thinking it was the cat, he walked to the foot of the stairs and called out, 'Here, puss, puss.' Anderson had picked up an axe on entering the house, and as his uncle came to the stairs he swung it, striking him with the blunt end of the blade and fracturing his skull. He then ransacked the house, taking almost £21 and some small items he thought he could pawn, as well as the raincoat. He had £14 hidden under his pillow at the time of his arrest and said he had spent the rest.

Willaim Anderson never recovered from his injuries and died at Durham County Hospital on 19 June. His great nephew was now charged with murder and, just three weeks later on 11 July, he found himself in the dock at Yorkshire Assizes, charged with the wilful murder of his uncle. The trial lasted two days and the jury took just one hour to consider their verdict. They added a recommendation for mercy, on account of his age.

Sentencing him to death, Mr Justice Croom-Johnson said that he did not concur with the recommendation to mercy and told the accused, 'You have been convicted on the very plainest of evidence. The best that can be said of you is that you have made a clean breast of it since your apprehension.'

There was no appeal and, examining the trial papers, the Home Secretary decided not to grant a reprieve. He noted on official papers that he had declined to show mercy as the prisoner was eighteen months older than the minimum age for execution, he had a criminal record, and the brutal battering of a blind old man marked it out as a very bad murder.

Nineteen-year-old Edward Walker Anderson was no stranger to the courts, but was probably surprised at the swift justice handed out to him. He was hanged just forty-two days after the brutal attack on his great uncle.

62

THE TROPHY KILLER

❖ *William Ambrose Collins, 28 October 1942* ❖

It was 8.30 on Saturday morning, 13 June 1942, when a milkman making his deliveries on Claremont Road, Town Moor, Newcastle saw something lying on the grass verge. Taking a closer look, he discovered the body of a woman, partially hidden behind a large emergency water pipe that was stored for the purpose of repairing bomb damage to the water mains.

Police were soon at the scene of the crime and the woman was quickly identified as Margaret Rice, a 24-year-old corporal in the WAAF. She had been sexually assaulted, raped and then battered to death. Items of her underclothing were missing.

Born in Essex, Margaret Rice lodged at Kenton, and, piecing together her last movements, police learned that her husband of almost two months, Lieutenant Patrick

The victim's body was discovered behind these emergency water pipes on Claremont Road, Newcastle. (Author's collection)

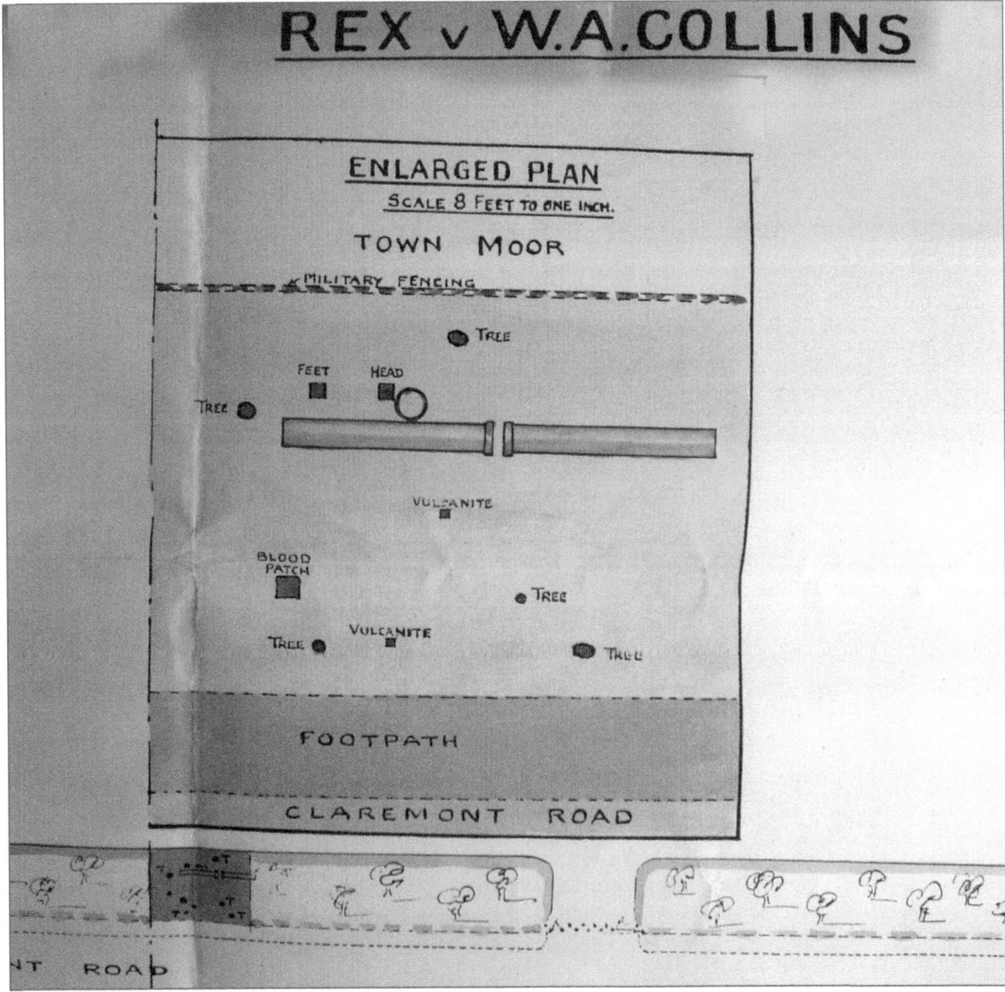

Police sketch of the murder scene, with the body and parts of the broken gun clearly marked. (Crime Picture Archive)

Rice, had been on leave with his wife in Newcastle. They had spent the previous night together, and in the early hours of Saturday morning Margaret had seen him off at Newcastle Central Station, as he was due to rejoin his unit.

At the crime scene, officers found two pieces of the vulcanite handle of a revolver, which suggested that Margaret had been battered with the handle of a gun. They also discovered that the body had been moved after death: small rivulets of blood were found flowing in the opposite direction to others close by. This suggested that the killer was most likely a local man, someone who was able to return to the murder scene after carrying out the attack, maybe to retrieve something he had lost or to collect a souvenir of his crime.

Witnesses at Newcastle station told police that they had seen two young men in the station buffet at the time and these two had left shortly after Margaret had waved off her

Margaret Rice. (T.J. Leech collection)

husband. Investigations into the men at the station led police to William Collins, a 21-year-old navy apprentice.

Collins was a single man with a criminal record for larceny, who lived at Framlington Place, close to Claremont Place, with his widowed mother. He admitted that he had been in the area at the time of the murder but was adamant that he had had nothing to do with the crime. He said he had been with a friend on the Friday evening, and that after visiting various pubs they ended up at Newcastle station at around 12.30 on Saturday morning. Collins's friend dropped him off on nearby Framlington Place, where the two men parted.

When Collins's story was checked, his friend told police that he had sold a Webley revolver to Collins on the Friday night. His house was searched, and beneath a pillow on his bed was a pair of women's knickers and a gun. The handle was damaged and the vulcanite pieces found at the murder scene matched perfectly. Collins was arrested and charged with murder. He then made a confession, claiming that he was drunk and that the attack had not been planned; he had happened upon the victim after being dropped off by his friend. He said that something seemed to come over him and before he realised what he was

Collins was hanged by uncle and nephew Tom and Albert Pierrepoint. (T.J. Leech archive/Author's collection)

H.M. Prison Durham.

28 October 1942.

Register No. 1103. Name William Ambrose Collins.

GENTLEMEN,

As directed in Standing Order No. 181, I have the honour to submit the annexed Record of the execution of the above-named Prisoner, which took place at 8-0 o'clock on the morning of the 28th October, 1942.

The Inquest was held on the same day, when the Jury returned the following verdict :—* Death was due to Dislocation of the Cervical Vertebrae due to execution of judgement of death by hanging for the murder of Margaret Mary Rice.

I am, Gentlemen,

Your obedient Servant,

To the Prison Commissioners,

W Foster

Governor.

Confirmation of the execution of William Ambrose Collins, 28 October 1942. (Author's collection)

doing it was too late. After committing the crime he had gone home but he later went back to check whether the girl was dead. Finding that she was, he then disposed of items of jewellery he had stolen from her by dropping them down a number of grids on the route home.

Before Mr Justice Cassels in August, the prosecution claimed that Collins was a sexual deviant, a trophy killer who had returned to the body to collect a sinister memento of the crime. Collins's defence argued that he was not responsible for his actions, referring to a cycle accident four years earlier in which he had sustained a head injury. The jury took just twenty minutes to decide that this was no defence to a brutal, sexually motivated crime.

63

MURDER AT THE AERODROME

❖ Sydney James Delasalle, 13 April 1944 ❖

Chingford-born Sydney Delasalle was a 39-year-old leading aircraftman serving at the RAF camp at Brunton aerodrome, Northumberland. He had previously served in the army from the age of 16 and had completed many terms of duty overseas. Delasalle had left the army in 1933, but was conscripted again in 1941.

On 2 February 1944, an inspection took place at the camp, headed by Flight Sergeant Ronald John Murphy. After an earlier inspection, Murphy had reported Delasalle concerning the state of his room. Now Delasalle began complaining to the sergeant about the rations, but his tone of voice was aggressive and he was warned that, if there was any further insolence, he would be taken to the station commander. Delasalle then invited the sergeant outside for a fight and as a result was confined to barracks.

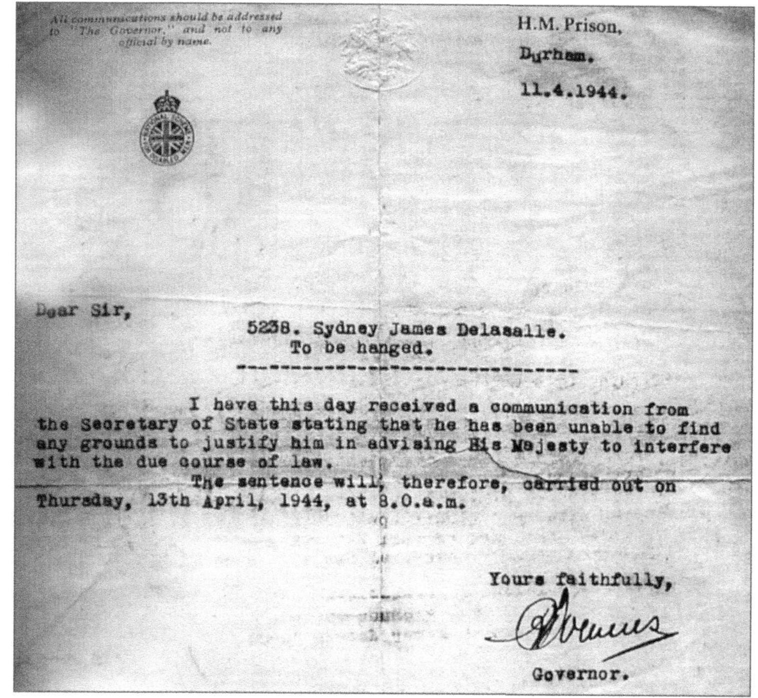

All communications should be addressed to "The Governor," and not to any official by name.

H.M. Prison,
Durham.
11.4.1944.

Dear Sir,

5238. Sydney James Delasalle.
To be hanged.

I have this day received a communication from the Secretary of State stating that he has been unable to find any grounds to justify him in advising His Majesty to interfere with the due course of law.

The sentence will, therefore, carried out on Thursday, 13th April, 1944, at 8.0.a.m.

Yours faithfully,

Governor.

Letter requesting the hangman's services. (Author's collection)

On 4 February, Delasalle was charged with insolence and sentenced to fourteen days' confinement to camp. As he left the station commander's office, he approached Murphy, who was queuing with colleagues for tea at a NAAFI van. Shouting for the other men to get out of the way, Delasalle pointed his gun and fired two shots into Murphy. The sergeant was killed instantly; four others were injured in the shooting.

At Delasalle's trial at Leeds on 22 March, before Mr Justice Hallett, the prosecution claimed that, when overpowered, he had stated that Murphy had asked for it, which showed premeditation and motive. Delasalle admitted that he resented the punishment he had received, but declared that he bore no malice against Murphy in particular.

The defence was insanity. According to Delasalle, he had no recollection of the crime until he realised he was being held down by some of the other men. A prison doctor testified that it was possible for Delasalle to have committed the crime in an automatic state and he would possibly have no memory of the crime afterwards.

Delasalle was a man of previous good character but evidence was heard that he did have a violent temper, a temper that caused him to lose control and commit a brutal murder.

64

THE WRONG GIRL

❖ Charles Edward Prescott, 5 March 1946 ❖

A deathly silence descended over the courtroom as the black cap was draped on to the wig of Mr Justice Lynskey. As the prisoner heard sentence of death passed on him, he looked across from the dock at his former sweetheart. Their eyes met, she grimaced and she slowly turned her head away. He bowed his head and stepped out of the dock down to the cells. As he disappeared from view, his mother, seated in the gallery, collapsed to the floor.

Charles Prescott was a 23-year-old Royal Marine commando from Biglands, near Wigton, Cumbria. In the autumn of 1945 he had deserted from his unit and returned home. He had been courting 18-year-old Isabelle 'Belle' Young for quite a while but their relationship had seemingly cooled. On 17 October 1945, he saw Belle with another man at a dance. In a jealous rage, Prescott made threats to shoot her and the man she was dancing with. A few days later, Belle told Prescott that she was ending their relationship, although she said she wished to remain friends, and told him he could write to her when he returned to camp.

Prescott took rejection badly. On 30 October, he met up with Belle, and when she again refused to rekindle their romance he pulled out a dagger and threatened to injure her. Belle was able to disarm him and throw the knife into a nearby field. As Prescott went to retrieve it, she quickly walked away.

Crummock Banks Farm in 1946. (Author's collection)

Isabelle 'Belle' Young poses for police photographer in the chair where her sister was shot dead on 19 November 1945. (TNA: PRO)

Death sentence on 'marine who 'shot wrong girl'

Sister's rejected lover denies threat to kill, and says gun went off accidentally

JUDGE AND JURY AGREE ON VERDICT OF SUPREME PENALTY FOR WAVERTON CRIME

SENTENCED TO DEATH for murdering the sister of the girl who had given him up, Marine Charles Edward Prescott stepped to the edge of the dock in Carlisle Assize Court on Thursday to look at Belle Young, the girl he loved.

There was a tense silence in the Court as his lips moved. The girl looked him in the eyes—and grimaced. Prescott bowed his head, hesitated a moment, and walked to the cells. His mother fainted and was carried from the court.

Prescott, whose home was at Biglands, near Wigton, told the Court that the shot that killed 19-year-old Sarah Jean Young was an accident. The gun went off when he was startled by a horse.

ALLEGED THREAT TO KILL.

For the prosecution it was stated

During the latter part of the time he was "squatting," accused con-

Mr. Gorman: I suggest you put it in in front of the Young's house on the night of Nov. 19. Can you deny that?—Accused: No.

And that you put it in to shoot in that house. Can you deny that?—Yes sir.

I suggest you put it in to carry out your threat to Belle Young.—No sir.

HAVE A SHOT AT RABBITS.

Can you think of any other reason why you put the cartridge in?—Th

Prescott's conviction made the headlines in Cumberland newspapers. (Author's collection)

On the night of 19 November there was a get-together at the Youngs' family home at Crummock Banks Farm, Waverton. Belle's 19-year-old sister, Sarah Jean, was showing some family photographs to Belle, their brother George and two workers at the farm when, as Sarah sat down beside one of the farmhands, a shot rang out. Sarah fell to the floor mortally wounded, a bullet having been fired through one of the farm windows.

One hour later, Prescott walked into a reading room at Waverton and, in front of several witnesses, announced that he had shot Belle Young. He calmly added that he hoped he had hit the right person, as there had been quite a crowd in the farmhouse and he had fired from more than 100 yards away. When the police arrived, Prescott ejected a cartridge from his rifle and placed it on the table. In his pockets he had another twenty-four rounds of ammunition.

At his trial, Prescott's defence was that the gun went off accidentally. He claimed that he had gone to the farm to see Belle and had tried to attract her attention by walking backwards and forwards near the windows. He left his rifle resting against a fence while he had a smoke. When a noise startled him, he swung round and the gun went off.

Asked why he was carrying a loaded rifle, Prescott said that he did not know it was loaded. He denied that he had made any statements in the reading room, despite testimony from the five witnesses. He also denied that he had told an officer on a previous occasion in November that he had waited behind a hedge for two days in order to 'do his girl in'.

Found guilty after a three-day trial, Prescott was the last man hanged at Durham by aged hangman Thomas Pierrepoint, entering his fortieth year as an executioner.

65

THE ETERNAL TRIANGLE

❖ Arthur Charles, 26 March 1946 ❖

In September 1945, black South Africans Arthur Charles and John Duplessis signed up together to serve on a ship berthed at Glasgow docks. Charles, a native of Durban, and Duplessis had both lived in England since the outbreak of the war, and during this time both had courted Mrs Hannah Burns at South Shields. Initially she had lived with Charles but when, in 1944, he found a position on a ship for several months, she moved in with Duplessis, the couple living together as man and wife. The two men had quarrelled about their relationships with Mrs Burns, but it seemed to have been resolved and they remained friends.

SHIELDS MURDER CHARGE AT ASSIZES

Arthur Charles (34), a native of South Africa, lodging in Dean Street, South Shields, was charged at Durham Assizes to-day with the murder of John Duplessis, also a coloured man and stated to be a shipmate of accused, at South Shields on November 29. Both men weresaid to be ship's firemen.

Dr. Charlesworth, prosecuting, said the case was that Charles shot Duplessis in cold blood. The latter lived with a woman named Hannah Burns, of Albemarle Street, South Shields. Accused had formerly lived with her, but was then in lodgings.

After describing how Mrs. Burns saw the two men in a public house on the night of November 29 Dr. Charlesworth said that Charles left after arranging to meet her at 10 o'clock.

Later at her house she saw accused with a revolver in his

News cutting reporting the murder of John Duplessis. (MCS archive)

On 28 November 1945, their ship arrived back in port and both men returned together to South Shields, where Duplessis spent the night with Mrs Burns at her home on Albemarle Street. On the following night, Duplessis and Hannah went out for a drink at the Locomotive Inn, and found Charles was also there drinking. The couple left the pub and went to a number of others, before ending the night at a café popular with sailors. Charles was also sitting there with a group of friends. As they drank a coffee, Duplessis and Mrs Burns were laughing, at which point Charles came over and accused them of laughing at him. Finishing their drinks, Hannah and Duplessis returned to Albemarle Street.

Duplessis retired to bed while Hannah washed the dishes. She went to pour out

	Tuesday. 26. March. 1946
Name	Arthur Charles 2494.
Age	34. years
Height.	5 . 5 3/4
Drop	8 . 2.
Weight.	134 lbs.
Remarks	Nigger murdered shipmate at Newcastle. upon. Tyne. Resistance but turned out a very good job. Steave's Wade's first job as senior executioner

Hangman's diary detailing the first execution carried out by Stephen Wade. (Author's collection)

the washing-up bowl in the grid outside and found herself face-to-face with Charles, who was carrying a gun. He pushed past her and stormed upstairs, challenging Duplessis to a fight. Seeing the gun, Duplessis declined the challenge, but when Charles persisted, Mrs Burns heard Duplessis say, 'Shoot if you are going to shoot.'

Six shots rang out. John Duplessis was seriously wounded, five bullets hitting their target. Charles was later arrested at his lodgings in Dean Street. He denied the shooting and

Hangman Stephen Wade. (Author's collection)

claimed not to own a gun. Furthermore, although he was identified by both Mrs Burns and Duplessis, who made a deposition from his hospital bed in the presence of Charles, he still maintained that it was a case of mistaken identity.

Charles was initially charged with attempted murder, but when Duplessis died from septicaemia on New Year's Eve, Charles found himself facing a murder charge. A few weeks later, a young boy playing near some railway arches on the route between Albemarle Street and Charles's lodgings found a rusty revolver that still contained six empty cartridge cases.

Charles was tried before Mr Justice Oliver at Durham Assizes on 14 February 1946. He denied the charges and insisted that it was a case of mistaken identity. Hannah Burns identified the gun as the one Charles had been carrying when he burst into the house and shot his former friend dead. The trial lasted just one day and, after a deliberation of two hours, the jury returned their guilty verdict.

Charles's execution marked the debut of hangman Stephen Wade as the 'number one', taking over from long-serving Tom Pierrepoint, who would be pensioned off by the Home Office within a few weeks.

66

A LOVER SPURNED

❖ *Benjamin Roberts, 13 December 1949* ❖

On the afternoon of Sunday 14 August 1949 three friends had tea together at Chilton Buildings, a prosperous mining village between Ferryhill and Darlington. They were 23-year-old Benny Roberts, his friend Alan Neal and Neal's attractive girlfriend, 21-year-old Lilian Vickers, all of whom had been friends since school. After the meal, Roberts showed them a shotgun he had been cleaning and which he claimed that he used to shoot rabbits.

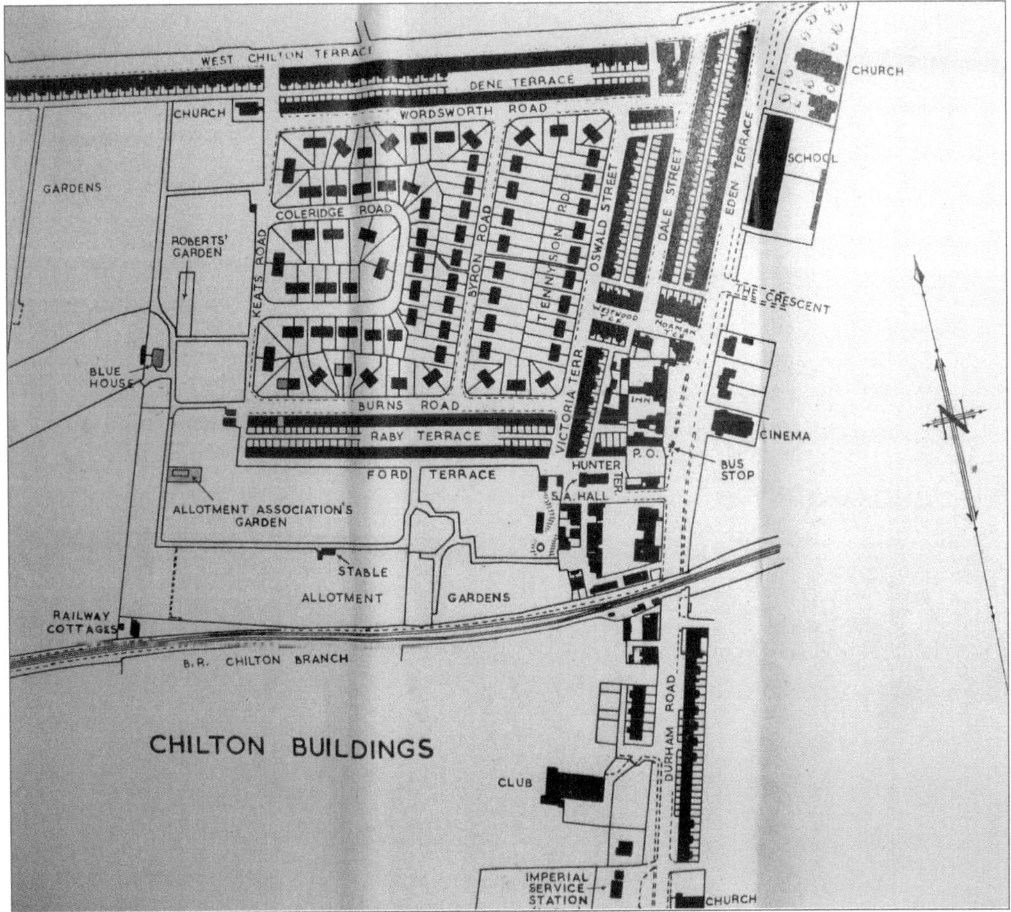

Police sketch of Chilton Buildings. (Crime Picture Archive)

Lilian had arranged to go to the cinema that night with a girlfriend, so they decided to meet up when she returned home. Neal and Roberts went out to the Eden Arms at Rushfield and met up with Lilian at 11 p.m. They returned to Roberts's house, where, after a drink Neal and Lilian left together.

As they kissed goodnight in the street, they noticed Roberts leave the house and head for the adjacent allotment garden. They decided to follow him through the garden but, reaching a hut, they lost sight of him. Moments later they heard footsteps and Roberts suddenly appeared, pointing the shotgun at them.

'What's the matter?' Neal asked. Without replying, Roberts simply pointed the gun. 'Don't be so soft, Benny,' Lilian said to him, at which point he pulled the trigger and she fell to the ground.

As Neal fled, a second then a third shot rang out. Neal rounded the corner and met up with Roberts's father, who had seen his son enter the allotments and gone to investigate. Together they returned to the hut and found Roberts lying on top of Lilian, having shot himself in the head.

Lilian Vickers was shot dead inside this hut. (Author's collection)

Chilton Buildings miner "Guilty" of murdering girl he loved

At Durham Assizes yesterday, Benjamin Roberts, aged 23, of Raby-terrace, Chilton Buildings, a miner, was found "Guilty" of the murder of 21-year-old Lilian Vickers, of Burns-road, Chilton Buildings, a laundry worker. The jury added a strong recommendation to mercy.

The case opened on Monday, and after an all-day hearing, Mr. Justice Oliver adjourned until yesterday when he gave his summing up.

The jury were out considering their verdict for an hour and ten minutes.

Heard sentence unmoved

was much attached to the girl and very disappointed about her attitude towards him.

Describing the tragedy the Judge said that Roberts had gone off his road which led to the railway and stood face to face with Neale and the girl with a loaded and cocked gun in his hand. If he was out to shoot rabbits by the railway why should he go after them?

But that was what he did, and Neale ... said ... "He appeared round the corner of the hut. He pointed the gun at both of us and said: 'Now then,' and I said: 'What is the matter, Benny,' and he said 'It is loaded.'

Roberts was found guilty at Durham Assizes. (MCS archive)

Roberts recovered from his injuries and stood trial before Mr Justice Oliver at Durham Assizes on 2 November. His story was that he had fired the gun without having any intention of shooting anyone, but as soon as he had seen Lilian fall, he had turned the gun upon himself. The prosecution claimed that it was wilful murder by a lover spurned, Roberts having decided that if he could not have the object of his desires, then no one else could.

67

THE ANIMAL

John Wilson, 13 December 1949

In the early hours of Sunday morning, 14 August 1949, John Wilson, a 26-year-old coal cutter of Murton Colliery, called at his sister's house and confessed that he had committed murder. Thinking he was drunk, she told him to go home. He then walked to his parents'

The body of Lucy Nightingale was concealed beneath these sheaves of corn. (Crime Picture Archive)

home at Cold Hesledon, County Durham, and in front of his father and brother repeated his claim. Convinced that he was telling the truth, they contacted the police.

When officers arrived at the house, Wilson handed over a wristwatch and ring that he said he had taken from the body. He told them that he had first met Lucy Nightingale, the 25-year-old wife of a seaman, in the King's Head at Easington on the previous Friday. They arranged to meet on the following day and together they had visited a number of pubs in the area before he walked her home.

He said that as they made their way across the fields, he went to kiss her. They headed towards a cornfield, when she started talking about money and demanded 10*s* before she would have sex with him. In a rage, he attacked her – like a wild animal, the detective who discovered the body later claimed – tore at her clothing and then raped her. The cause of death was strangulation. Wilson then covered the body with sheaves of corn before calling at a nearby pub, where, after a glass of rum, he decided to confess to his sister.

His trial before Mr Justice Oliver at Durham Assizes on 2 November was a formality, his confession to the police prior to his arrest effectively sealing his fate. John Wilson was hanged alongside Benny Roberts in the last double execution to take place at Durham Gaol.

68

THE NORTH SHIELDS STRANGLER

❖ *George Finlay Brown, 11 July 1950* ❖

It was shortly before 11 p.m. on Friday 10 March 1950 when neighbours heard heavy footsteps on the stairs leading to a flat in King Street, North Shields, the home of Mrs Mary Victoria Longhurst. Moments later, a scream rang out, followed by shouting and another scream. Finally they heard the sound of someone running fast down the stairs.

The police were called and, entering her room, they found the body of 23-year-old Mrs Longhurst. She was lying on the metal frame bed with her head at the bottom and her feet on the pillow. She had been strangled and the ligature used was tied to the foot of the bed.

Detectives learned that Mrs Longhurst was separated from her husband and young child and had taken lodgings at King Street. It was known that she had been dating a young labourer, 23-year-old George Finlay Brown, until March, when she had ended the relationship and taken up with another man.

IN THE COURT OF CRIMINAL APPEAL
CRIMINAL APPEAL ACT, 1907

NOTIFICATION OF RESULT OF APPLICATION TO THE FULL COURT

REX v. **GEORGE FINLAY BROWN** (Appellant)

H.M. Prison **DURHAM**

THIS IS TO GIVE YOU NOTICE that the Court of Criminal Appeal, as duly constituted for the hearing of Appeals under the Act, has this day considered the Application of the above-named Appellant for:-

(a) Extension of the time within which Notice of Appeal or application for leave to Appeal may be given;

(b) Leave to appeal against **conviction**

(c) Legal aid;

(d) Permission to be present during the proceedings in the Appeal;

(e) Bail;

(f) Leave to call further evidence -

and has determined the same, and has refused them

Dated this 26 day of **JUNE** A.D. 194 **1950**

A. HIGHMORE KING,
Registrar of the Court of Criminal Appeal

To His Majesty's Principal Secretary of State for the Home Department
To the Prison Commissioners
To the Governor of His Majesty's Prison at
To the Clerk of the Assize.
To the above-named Appellant

DS 79198/2/303 2m 11/48 PL

Official notification that George Finlay Brown's appeal had been rejected. (Author's collection)

Brown and Mary had been seen arguing in the street on the previous day, but they had settled their differences and spent the night together at Mary's house. On the following day they began to argue again, to the extent that Mary went to the police station and made a complaint against Brown. He was interviewed by officers and warned to stay away from King Street.

King Street, North Shields, 1950. Mary Longhurst had a flat in the building to the left of the street lamp. (Author's collection)

When Brown was picked up by detectives, he claimed that he had not been anywhere near King Street on the night of the murder. He said he had visited a pub and then gone for a long walk before returning home. Although witnesses placed him in the pub earlier in the evening, there was no one to support his alibi for the time of the murder, and witnesses testified to seeing him close to the house shortly before the murder.

Brown was sentenced to death by Mr Justice Morris at Northumberland Assizes in Newcastle on 31 May, the jury deliberating a verdict for thirty minutes. His appeal failed and Brown was duly hanged. His execution was notable in that it was the only time the well-known hangman Albert Pierrepoint officiated at Durham Gaol.

69

A STRANGE AFFAIR

❖ *John Walker, 13 July 1950* ❖

Francis and Gladys Wilson married in 1944 and settled in a home at Station Road, Brompton, near Northallerton. It did not take Gladys long to realise that she had made the wrong choice for a husband and she began a relationship with a soldier, John Walker.

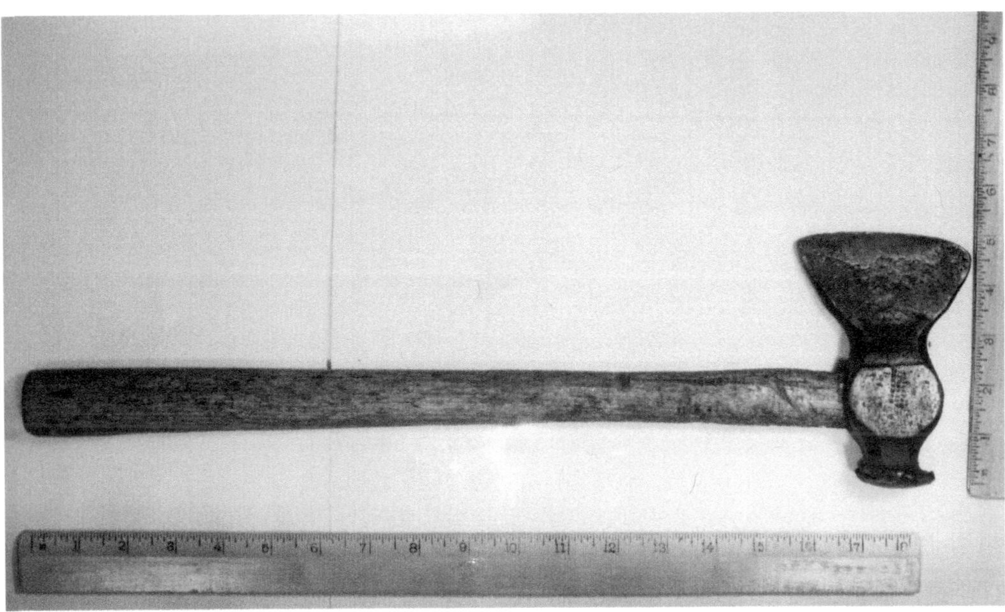

The axe John Walker used to batter Francis Wilson to death. (Author's collection)

Francis Wilson was battered to death in the scullery at his home on Station Road, Brompton. (TNA: PRO)

In 1947, following his demob from the army, Walker found work as a labourer and moved in with Gladys and her husband as a lodger. It was a strange affair: the two men soon swapped roles. Walker began to share a bed with Gladys, with the blessing of her husband, who now occupied the spare room. Although he seemed content with this arrangement, Wilson was often violent to his wife, although less so when Walker was around.

On 29 April 1950, there was an argument between Wilson and his wife over some money. It was Gladys's custom to give her husband 10s each week for him to spend on himself, but on this occasion she only gave him half that amount. That evening, while Gladys was at the cinema, Wilson made a remark to the effect that next time he was alone with Gladys, he would give her a good hiding: 'When I get her on her own, I will knock the living daylights out of her,' he boasted.

Gladys returned at eleven o'clock that night. Walker was still up, but there was no sign of her husband. At 6.30 on the following morning, Walker woke Gladys with a cup of tea and told her that he would have to go away, as her husband was lying dead in the kitchen. He said that he had killed Francis when he had threatened to attack her with an axe. Walker then left the house and cycled towards Darlington.

Wilson's body was discovered in the small scullery at the back of the kitchen. He had been struck six times with a heavy axe, which was found lying beside the body. Walker was arrested later that day in Bishop Auckland.

Walker, who stood just 5ft tall, never denied the crime, but claimed that he had done it to prevent the murder of the woman he loved. The prosecution coldly argued that, whatever the reason for the crime, it was still a cold-blooded murder. On 22 June 1950 at York Assizes, Mr Justice Croom-Johnson sentenced John Walker to death. There was no appeal and his execution took place just two days after that of George Finlay Brown.

70

DEATH WISH

❖ *Patrick Turnage, 14 November 1950* ❖

It was shame that led to Patrick Turnage making an eight o'clock appointment with hangman Steve Wade on a cold November morning in 1950. Turnage, an Indian-born sailor, had chosen the unusual step of pleading guilty at his Durham Assizes trial, even though his counsel told him that a manslaughter verdict was the most likely outcome and he would face just a term in jail, rather than the hangman's rope.

On the afternoon of 30 July, the body of 78-year-old Mrs Julia Beesley was found at Billingham Wharf, Teesside. She had been strangled and dumped in bushes close to where the SS *Absalon* was moored. On the previous evening, Turnage had caught the bus into

Photograph of the SS Absalon *taken on the day Patrick Turnage was arrested.* (Author's collection)

town, where he was advised by a bus conductor that the most likely place to pick up a woman was the Victoria Hotel in Joseph Street.

Turnage got into conversation with Julia Beesley, who, despite her age, still worked as a prostitute, and when he suggested that they go back to his ship, where they could have a few more drinks, she agreed. They took a taxi back and, as he paid the fare, Turnage told the driver not to wait as the woman would be staying all night.

A crew member on duty saw the taxi pull away and watched the couple move towards the ship. They stopped and, following raised voices, the woman stormed off in the direction of the departed taxi. Turnage watched for a moment and then followed her.

Julia Beesley was reported missing on the following morning, and at two o'clock that afternoon her body was found. She had been strangled. Turnage was recognised as the man seen in the company of the old woman, heading towards his ship, and he was arrested just a few hours before the *Absalon* was due to set sail.

Questioned by detectives, Turnage made no attempt to deny that he had been with Julia and handed over her handbag to the police. He strenuously denied murder and claimed that they had argued over sex and he had pushed her into the ditch. He had not deliberately strangled her. Indeed, the post-mortem suggested that death could have been caused by the simple act of tightening the clothing around Julia's neck.

Although Turnage was charged with murder, it seemed unlikely that there was enough evidence to secure a conviction when, on 26 October, just two days before the case was due to come to court, Turnage asked to see Detective Chief Inspector Rowell and informed him that he wished to plead guilty to the charge of murder. He said that he knew what he was doing and also that he had known that Julia was dead when he left her.

When the case came to court before Mr Justice Hallett in October, Turnage repeated his guilty plea. Chief Inspector Rowell was called to give evidence, and relayed the brief details of the crime and the conversation with Turnage. There was no further evidence, the plea was accepted and Turnage was sentenced to death. The entire proceedings took just seven minutes.

71

DEATH OF A MISTRESS

❖ Tahir Ali, 21 March 1952 ❖

For six and a half years, Evelyn McDonald, a 25-year-old prostitute, had been living with Montez Ullah, an Indian seaman, at Adelaide Street, South Shields, but during one of Ullah's trips to sea, she moved in with his cousin, Tahir Ali.

Evelyn McDonald was stabbed to death in front of the metal gates. (Author's collection)

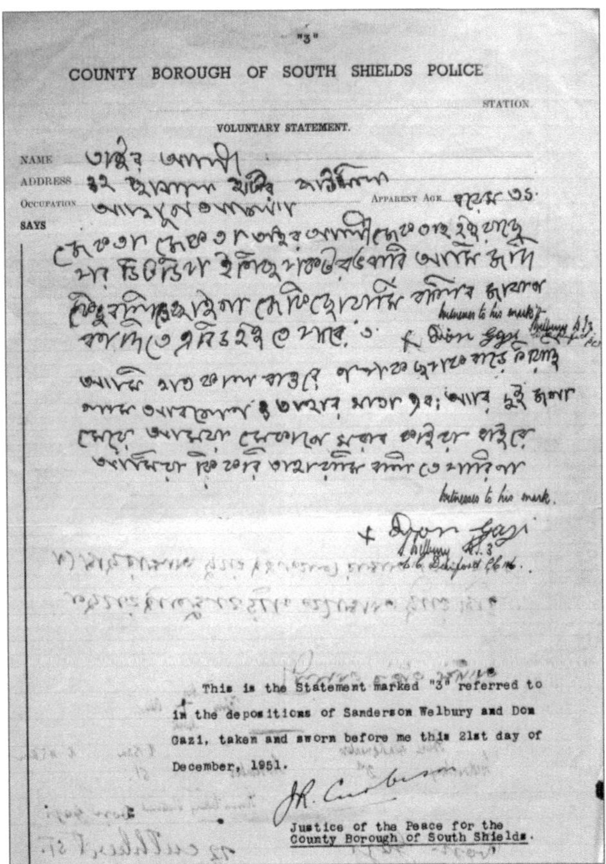

"3"

COUNTY BOROUGH OF SOUTH SHIELDS POLICE

STATION

VOLUNTARY STATEMENT.

NAME

ADDRESS

OCCUPATION

APPARENT AGE

SAYS

This is the Statement marked "3" referred to in the depositions of Sanderson Welbury and Dom Gazi, taken and sworn before me this 21st day of December, 1951.

Justice of the Peace for the County Borough of South Shields.

Tahir Ali made his first statement in the early hours of Wednesday 21 November 1951. (TNA: PRO)

Tahir Ali was a 40-year-old seagoing fireman, who lived at Saville Street, South Shields. Although he was happily married with a wife and children in his native East Pakistan, he took Evelyn as his mistress and began to spend money on her freely.

He was therefore somewhat put out when, on his next voyage, Evelyn returned to live with Ullah. Also moving into the house was Evelyn's friend Mary Lucas. In early November 1951 there was an argument between Ali and Evelyn, which only ended when Mary Lucas had to separate them. In a rage, Ali said that he would kill Evelyn, and if Mary got in the way, he would kill her too.

On the evening of Tuesday 20 November, Evelyn and Mary went to a local pub, where Ali and Evelyn's mother later joined them. Her mother left at 10 p.m., and as the remaining three left the pub, Ali told Mary he wanted to go home with her. She refused and a struggle broke out, during which Ali pulled out a wicked-looking flick-knife and stabbed Evelyn three times. Quickly placed under arrest, Ali told detectives that he had spent over £500 on her, and killed her because she had made a fool of him.

Following a two-day trial before Mr Justice Hallett, the jury needed just thirty-five minutes to return a guilty verdict. Although the local Muslim population petitioned the prime minister of Pakistan, it failed to save Ali from the gallows.

72

JUMPING TO THE WRONG CONCLUSION

❖ *Herbert Appleby, 24 December 1952* ❖

It was the early hours of Sunday 21 September 1952 when a taxi pulled up outside South Bank police station at Grangetown, near Middlesbrough. Two young men walked through the door and the taxi driver told the desk sergeant, 'There is a man outside in my cab who says he has stabbed a man.' Sergeant Ellis left the station and spoke to the man in the cab, asking if it was true.

'I have stabbed a man. And that is that. He pinched my girl,' he said, before bursting into tears. He was cautioned and then made a full statement. He gave his name as Herbert Appleby of Laing Street, Grangetown, and said he had committed the murder during a party. Ellis checked out the story, learning that a man had been found to be dead on arrival at Middlesbrough Hospital in the last hour. When detectives interviewed Appleby, the events leading up to the tragedy were explained.

Herbert Appleby, the second of two men hanged at Christmas Eve at Durham Gaol. (Author's collection)

Appleby told them that he had been a groomsman at the wedding of a friend and the tragedy had taken place after the couple had departed for their honeymoon. After closing time, the guests had returned to the home of another guest. Twenty-year-old Appleby, a sling loader at the local docks, had attended with his girlfriend, 20-year-old Lillian 'Dolly' Robbins. When Appleby, who had been talking with some workmates, went in search of Dolly, he found her sitting on the sofa with 29-year-old John David Thomas, a fitter at the shipyard, and the stepbrother of the bridegroom. What enraged Appleby was that Thomas had his arm around Dolly's waist.

Appleby jumped to the conclusion that Dolly had ditched him and taken up with Thomas. He stormed from the room and walked the 200 yards to his home, where, in a rage, he picked up a carving knife and headed back to the party.

Thomas was still sitting next to Dolly when Appleby returned. Appleby walked up to him with the knife in his hand. There was nothing untoward going on but, without waiting for an explanation, Appleby said, 'I have brought this for you,' stabbing him once in the chest. As blood oozed from the wound, Appleby ran outside. He was joined by a workmate, to whom he said, 'You'd better fetch the police. He is dead. I shall hang.' They were sadly prophetic words.

Appleby's defence at his trial before Mr Justice Cassels, at Leeds Assizes at the beginning of December, was that he was insane at the time of the murder. Despite having confessed to police almost at once, he entered a plea of not guilty. Witnesses testified that he had left the house and returned with a knife, which suggested premeditation, and although it was shown that he was drunk at the time, this was to be no defence to a charge of murder.

Following the inevitable guilty verdict, Appleby's father immediately launched a petition. Among the first to sign was his girlfriend, Dolly Robbins. There was no appeal against the conviction, all hopes being pinned on the sentence being commuted. The execution was fixed for Christmas Eve 1952 and, as efforts to stall the execution failed, Appleby kept a brave face in the death cell.

As the fateful hour struck, Herbert Appleby, the man who had jumped to the wrong conclusion about his girlfriend, with dreadful consequences, thanked the prison staff for their kindness and walked bravely on to the drop.

73

THE HOMICIDE ACT

❖ *John Willson Vickers, 23 July 1957* ❖

The general store on Tait Street, Carlisle seemed an easy target. Jane Duckett, a 72-year-old spinster, lived alone above the shop and was partially deaf. The plan was simple. John Vickers, a 22-year-old petty thief, had it all worked out. He would break in, steal the money he knew she kept in the basement and make his escape.

At two o'clock on the morning of Monday 15 April 1957, Vickers carried out his plan, gaining entry into the shop and heading straight for the cellar. There were, however, just a couple of slight problems.

First, the money was not as easy to get at as he had surmised; and second, Jane Duckett was not as deaf as Vickers had been led to believe. As he rummaged through the darkened cellar, she heard the disturbance and, dressed only in her nightgown, descended the stairs to investigate. Hearing her footsteps, Vickers hid behind the stairs, hoping that she would

not see him. Problem number three began when she discovered the intruder, raised her arms and charged at him, fists flailing wildly.

Vickers panicked. He struck out, hitting the old lady several blows, and as she slumped on the floor, he kicked her a number of times in the face before ransacking the house in a vain search for the money. He fled empty-handed and Jane Duckett died from her injuries a few hours later.

The petty criminal was well known to the police and detectives soon tracked him down. Vickers damned himself in his opening statement. He admitted entering the premises in order to carry out a robbery, and although he admitted striking the woman, he claimed it was in self-defence and that he did not intend to kill her. The scratches on his face supported his story that the old lady had attacked him. Three days after the murder, detectives had a man in custody and he had made a statement admitting his involvement in the crime.

Tried before Mr Justice Hinchcliffe at Cumberland Assizes on 23 May, Vickers faced a charge of capital murder. There had been no executions in Great Britain since August 1955 and, after a lengthy debate, Parliament had brought in the Homicide Act. This Act categorised certain types of murder and classified them as either

Mrs Jane Duckett. (MCS archive)

The general store on Tait Street, Carlisle. (Author's collection)

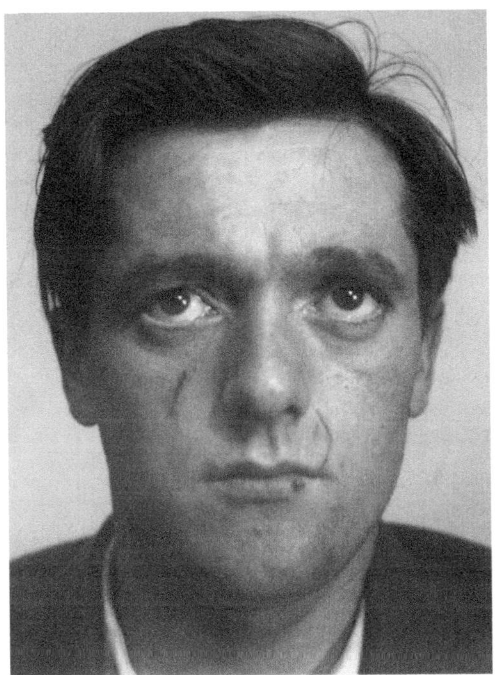

John Willson Vickers. (Author's collection)

Scene-of-crime photograph of the murder of Mrs Duckett. (TNA: PRO)

capital or non-capital murder. Only capital murder now carried the death penalty and Section Five covered the killing of a person while in the furtherance of theft. It had become law on 21 March 1957.

Vickers's defence argued that, as no theft had actually taken place, it should be a lesser charge of non-capital murder. It now came down to interpretation of the law. The prosecution claimed that, as Vickers had admitted that he had entered the premises to steal, the killing had therefore indeed been in the furtherance of theft.

Vickers was duly convicted of capital murder and sentenced to death. However, the verdict now raised a point of law. The new Act seemed to imply that if there was no malice aforethought, it could not be murder. The original appeal court thought this point of law so crucial that they adjourned the appeal and re-sat with a panel of five instead of the customary three judges.

Assistant Harry Smith and chief hangman Harry Allen carried out the execution of Vickers in July 1957. It was the first execution under the new Homicide Act. (Author's collection)

All Communications
to be addressed to
G. L. S. LIGHTFOOT,
UNDER SHERIFF

TEL. NOS.—22525-6
YOUR REF.:
MY REF.: GLSL

UNDER SHERIFF'S O
21 CASTLE STREE
CARLISLE

9th July, 1957

Dear Sir,

3900 John Willson Vickers
Capital Murder

With reference to my letter dated 3rd June, I have now been informed that the Court of Criminal Appeal has dismissed the prisoner's appeal.

In these circumstances the High Sheriff of Cumberland has fixed the execution for Tuesday 23rd July 1957 at 9 a.m. at Durham Prison and I shall be glad to know that you can undertake the duties of executioner. On this assumption, I enclose two copies of a Memorandum of Conditions to which any person acting as executioner is required to conform. On the back of one copy is an acknowledgment that you have received it. I shall be glad if you will sign and date this acknowledgment and return it to me in the enclosed stamped addressed envelope.

Provided there is no reprieve the High Sheriff and myself will be arriving at the prison on the afternoon of 22nd July and no doubt I shall have an opportunity of seeing you in order to ascertain that everything is in order.

Should there be a reprieve I shall at once notify you by telegram when the matter will, of course, be cancelled.

Yours faithfully,

Mr H.B. Allen,
Junction Hotel,
Whitefield,
Nr. Manchester.

Letter confirming that the execution would go ahead. (Author's collection)

At the dismissal of the appeal, it was explained that where the accused inflicted grievous bodily harm in the furtherance of another offence, such as robbery, and that violence led to death, the person was guilty of capital murder. The defence sought to appeal to the House of Lords, but permission was refused.

Vickers was not the first man to be sentenced to death under this new act: Ronald Patrick Dunbar of Newcastle-upon-Tyne claimed that dubious honour, having been sentenced to death on 16 May. Dunbar had occupied the same condemned cell at Durham that was later to house Vickers, but his sentence was commuted to life imprisonment. John Willson Vickers was not so lucky: he was hanged on Tuesday 23 July. It was the first execution carried out under the Homicide Act.

74

CAPITAL MURDER?

❖ *Frank Stokes, 3 September 1958* ❖

Detectives in Northumberland County Constabulary initially wondered if it was the work of a serial killer. On 14 April 1958, 75-year-old widow Mrs Linda Violet Ash was admitted to hospital with severe head injuries and died on the following day. She had

Wanted
Man to look after small garden, able to grow flowers, can work in spare time if more suitable
Apply 41. Marlborough Avenue.
Gosforth.

Frank Stokes replied to this advert placed by Mrs Ash *in April 1958.* (Author's collection)

Marlborough Ave, Gosforth in 1958. (Author's collection)

been attacked with a hammer in her home on Marlborough Avenue, Gosforth, in Northumberland. It was the second murder in the area in forty-eight hours.

Neighbours were able to give police the description of a man who, on the day of the attack, had asked directions to Mrs Ash's house. This matched a description given by Mrs Tate, a lodger of Mrs Ash, who had answered the door to the caller, and had left the man talking to Violet on the doorstep. It was she who had discovered Mrs Ash lying unconscious when she returned home a short time later.

Chief Superintendent Patterson was put in charge of the case and, after quickly dismissing links to the earlier Gosforth murder, announced that he wished to interview a man who had responded to an advert for a gardener, placed in a corner shop by Mrs Ash.

On 25 April, 44-year-old Frank Stokes, an unemployed hotel porter from Leeds, walked into London's Cannon Row police station and told the officer on the desk that he had murdered a woman. Cautioned, he made a full confession to the killing of Mrs Ash.

He explained that he had answered her advertisement for a gardener and had asked for 4*s* an hour. She had given him a hammer and told him that he could have the job but she would pay him only 3*s* 6*d*. He then lost his temper and started hitting her. He said the motive for the killing was not theft, but anger at her offer of employment. Crucially, he denied stealing from her house.

Stokes stood accused of capital murder – in the furtherance of theft – on 23 July at Yorkshire Assizes, Leeds, before Mr Justice Davies. He entered a plea of guilty to non-capital murder. The prosecution rejected this plea, mainly because, when searched by the police following his arrest, Stokes was in possession of a purse, which contained a number of bank notes. Stokes claimed that he had also answered a similar advertisement for a gardener at Ewell in Surrey, and it was from there that he had stolen the purse.

The prosecution claimed that the purse was in fact the property of Mrs Ash and that by stealing it he had committed capital murder. Stokes's defence countered that he had taken nothing from the house at Gosforth, apart from the key that he had used to lock the door, and, as he had stolen nothing, the crime was not a capital offence.

The prosecution argued that the fact that Stokes had already admitted that he had stolen from the Surrey house while engaged as a gardener supported their claim that he had carried out theft at Gosforth. After a three-day trial, Stokes was found guilty of capital murder and sentenced to death.

75

THE DESERTER

❖ *Brian Chandler, 17 December 1958* ❖

Having deserted from his unit at Catterick military hospital, 20-year-old private Brian Chandler of the Royal Army Medical Corps now needed money. It was Sunday 8 June 1958 and, slipping away from Catterick, he headed back to his native Middlesbrough. En route, Chandler reasoned that the military police would probably head straight for his hometown, so he instead alighted at Darlington. Here he met up with two teenage girls, Marian Munro and Pauline Blair, who had both run away from home.

The three of them spent the following night in a caravan on the outskirts of Darlington with another soldier. On the following morning, the soldier returned to his unit and Chandler and the girls now discussed how they could obtain enough money to travel down to London.

Marian told him of Martha Dodd, an 83-year-old woman she had once worked for. Chandler decided she would be an easy target and on 10 June the three of them visited Martha at her home on Victoria Road. Marian asked if there was any work available and Martha told them that if they came back tomorrow, she might have some jobs for them.

They decided to return on the following day if they were unable to obtain any money in the meantime. Later that afternoon, Pauline's mother appeared and took her daughter home. When Chandler was unable to find a buyer for a bicycle he stole that afternoon, he decided that they would go ahead with their plan to rob the old lady. With her friend now gone, Marian began to worry about the implications of what she had agreed to and expressed her concerns that the old woman would recognise her and inform the police. She said later that Chandler had callously claimed if she did, he would kill her.

Brian Chandler, the last man to be hanged at Durham. (Author's collection)

Scene-of-crime photograph of the murder of Martha Dodd. (TNA: PRO)

Victoria Road, Darlington in 1958. (Author's collection)

The following morning they parted for a few hours as Marian had an appointment at the labour exchange. At 3.30 that afternoon, in the company of some friends, she met Chandler outside the Royal cinema. He was smoking a cigarette, and when Marian asked how he had found the money to buy cigarettes, he told her that he had killed a woman. They could all see that Chandler had bloodstains on his trousers.

Chandler and Marian spent that Wednesday night at the house of a Mr and Mrs Hill. In the meantime, the body of Martha Dodd was discovered. She had been brutally battered to death, with nineteen separate wounds being inflicted on her, twelve to the head. The murder made the morning papers, which mentioned that the police wished to speak to the young deserter. Hill told Chandler that the police were looking for him and accompanied him to the station. Chandler initially denied the crime but, left alone for several hours to ponder his fate, he summoned detectives to his cell. 'I wish to get it off my chest,' he told them. He then gave his account of what had happened that afternoon.

He claimed that he had gone to the house of Martha Dodd to offer her his services as a gardener. She had agreed to his request and given him a bucket, which contained a hammer. In echoes of the Stokes case from earlier that year, he then stated that she had offered him just 3s an hour, and when he said that he wanted more money, Martha had lost her temper, seized the hammer and attacked him with it. He had only hit out to protect himself. The fact that the victim had received nineteen heavy blows convinced detectives that the story was far from the truth and he was charged with capital murder.

When the case came to trial at Durham Assizes before Mr Justice Ashworth, Chandler

Hangman Robert Leslie 'Jock' Stewart. (Author's collection)

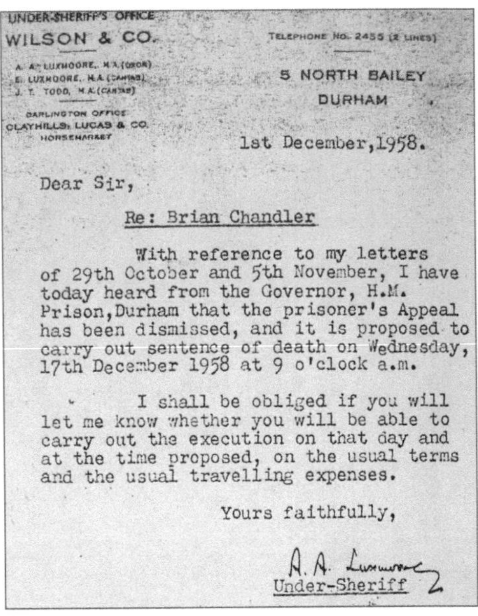

UNDER-SHERIFF'S OFFICE
WILSON & CO.
A. A. LUXMOORE, M.A. (OXON)
E. LUXMOORE, M.A. (CANTAB)
J. T. TODD, M.A. (CANTAB)
DARLINGTON OFFICE
CLAYHILLS, LUCAS & CO.
HORSEMARKET

TELEPHONE No. 2455 (2 LINES)
5 NORTH BAILEY
DURHAM

1st December, 1958.

Dear Sir,

Re: Brian Chandler

With reference to my letters of 29th October and 5th November, I have today heard from the Governor, H.M. Prison, Durham that the prisoner's Appeal has been dismissed, and it is proposed to carry out sentence of death on Wednesday, 17th December 1958 at 9 o'clock a.m.

I shall be obliged if you will let me know whether you will be able to carry out the execution on that day and at the time proposed, on the usual terms and the usual travelling expenses.

Yours faithfully,

A. A. Luxmoore
Under-Sheriff

Letter sent to the hangman requesting his services at the last execution to take place at Durham Gaol. (Author's collection) changed his story. In this new version of events, he claimed that he had found Martha already dead when he had called at the house and that Marian Munro was standing over the body.

The jury took less than two hours to return a verdict of guilty of capital murder, believing that Chandler alone had deliberately carried out a brutal murder in the pursuance of theft.

Chandler, a strapping 6-footer, was not expected to go to the gallows without a fight, and extra guards were placed on standby. In the event, these fears were ungrounded. Hangman 'Jock' Stewart noted that Chandler had his eyes tightly shut as he was led the few short paces to the drop. Seconds later, Brian Chandler, the last man to be hanged at Durham Gaol, was dead.

Appendix I

PUBLIC EXECUTIONS AT DRYBURN 1802–5

Date of Execution	*Convict*	*Executioner(s)*	*Crime*
23 August 1802	John Castleton	William Curry*	Attempted murder
15 August 1803	John Moses	William Curry*	Burglary
12 August 1805	Richard Metcalfe	William Curry*	Murder of son-in-law

Appendix II

PUBLIC EXECUTIONS OUTSIDE DURHAM GAOL 1816–65

Date of Execution	*Convict*	*Executioner(s)*	*Crime*
17 August 1816	John Greig	William Curry	Murder of Elizabeth Stonehouse
12 April 1819	George Atcheson (68)	William Curry	Rape of Isabella Ramshaw, a child
16 August 1819	John King (19)	William Curry	Murder of James Hamilton
18 March 1822	Henry Anderson	William Curry	Rape of Sarah Armstrong
9 August 1822	Robert Peat (50)	William Curry	Murder of Robert Peat, a relative
28 February 1831	Thomas Clarke (19)	William Curry	Murder of Mary Ann Westhorpe
3 August 1832	William Jobling	William Curry	Murder of Nicholas Fairles
16 August 1839	Jacob Ehlert (27)	William Calcraft*	Murder of Captain John Berkholtz
25 March 1848	William Thompson (27)	Nathaniel Howard	Murder of John Shirley
11 August 1859	John Wilthew (51)	Thomas Askern	Murder of his wife
27 December 1860	Milner Lockney (58)	Thomas Askern	Murder of Thomas Harrison
27 December 1860	Thomas Smith (35)	Thomas Askern	Murder of John Baty
23 December 1862	John Cox (25)	Thomas Askern	Murder of Anne Halliday
16 March 1865	Matthew Atkinson (41)	Thomas Askern	Murder of his wife

* Probable, although not recorded.

Appendix III

PRIVATE EXECUTIONS INSIDE DURHAM GAOL 1869–1958

Date of Execution	*Convict*	*Executioner*	*Assistant(s)*
22 March 1869	John Dolan John McConville	William Calcraft	
13 January 1873	John Hayes Hugh Slane	William Calcraft	
24 March 1873	Mary Cotton	William Calcraft	Robert Evans
5 January 1874	Charles Dawson Edward Gough William Thompson	William Marwood	
28 December 1874	Hugh Daley	William Marwood	
2 August 1875	Michael Gillingham William McHugh Elizabeth Pearson	William Marwood	
26 July 1876	John Williams	William Marwood	
30 July 1878	Robert Vest	William Marwood	
16 November 1880	William Brownless	William Marwood	
16 May 1882	Thomas Fury	William Marwood	
6 August 1883	James Burton	William Marwood	
24 November 1883	Peter Bray	Bartholomew Binns	
28 May 1884	Joseph Lowson	James Berry	
18 December 1888	William Waddell	James Berry	
22 December 1891	John Johnson	James Billington	
22 March 1898	Charles Smith	James Billington	Thomas Billington
12 December 1900	John Bowes	James Billington	William Billington
10 December 1901	John Thompson	William Billington	John Billington
16 December 1902	Thomas Nicholson Thomas Walton	William Billington	John Billington
8 December 1903	James Duffy	William Billington	John Billington
2 August 1904	George Breeze	John Billington	John Ellis
24 March 1908	Robert W. Lawman Joseph Noble	Henry Pierrepoint	Thomas Pierrepoint
5 August 1908	Matthew James Dodds	Henry Pierrepoint	Thomas Pierrepoint
23 February 1909	Jeremiah O'Connor	Henry Pierrepoint	Thomas Pierrepoint
8 December 1909	Abel Atherton	Henry Pierrepoint	William Willis
12 July 1910	Thomas Craig	Henry Pierrepoint	William Willis
24 March 1914	Robert Upton	John Ellis	William Willis
11 August 1915	Frank Steele	John Ellis	Robert Baxter

Date of Execution	*Convict*	*Executioner*	*Assistant(s)*
20 December 1916	Joseph Deans	John Ellis	George Brown
23 March 1920	William Hall	John Ellis	Robert Baxter
30 November 1920	James Riley	Thomas Pierrepoint	Edward Taylor
21 March 1922	James Williamson	Thomas Pierrepoint	William Willis
3 April 1923	Daniel Cassidy	Thomas Pierrepoint	Robert Wilson
8 August 1923	Hassan Muhamed	Thomas Pierrepoint	Robert Wilson
2 January 1924	Matthew F. A. Nunn	Thomas Pierrepoint	Thomas Phillips
15 April 1925	Henry Graham	Thomas Pierrepoint	Robert Wilson
	Thomas Shelton		William Willis
			Thomas Phillips
10 August 1926	James Smith	Thomas Pierrepoint	Thomas Phillips
6 January 1928	John Thomas Dunn	Thomas Pierrepoint	Thomas Phillips
10 August 1928	Norman Elliott	Thomas Pierrepoint	Robert Wilson
4 January 1929	Charles Conlin	Thomas Pierrepoint	Frank Rowe
7 August 1929	James Johnson	Thomas Pierrepoint	Thomas Phillips
6 December 1933	Ernest Wadge Parker	Thomas Pierrepoint	Alfred Allen
9 May 1935	John S. Bainbridge	Thomas Pierrepoint	Henry Pollard
16 July 1935	George Hague	Thomas Pierrepoint	Stanley Cross
16 December 1936	Christopher Jackson	Thomas Pierrepoint	Albert Pierrepoint
26 May 1938	Robert W. Hoolhouse	Thomas Pierrepoint	
26 July 1938	William Parker	Thomas Pierrepoint	Thomas Phillips
8 February 1939	John Daymond	Thomas Pierrepoint	Robert Wilson
			Alex Riley (trainee observer)
11 July 1940	William Appleby	Thomas Pierrepoint	Albert Pierrepoint
	Vincent Ostler		Stanley Cross
			Alex Riley
10 September 1940	John Wright	Thomas Pierrepoint	Albert Pierrepoint
24 December 1940	Edward Scollen	Thomas Pierrepoint	Henry Critchell
6 March 1941	Henry Lyndo White	Thomas Pierrepoint	Harry B. Allen
31 July 1941	Edward W. Anderson	Thomas Pierrepoint	Herbert Morris
28 October 1942	William A. Collins	Thomas Pierrepoint	Albert Pierrepoint
13 April 1944	Sydney J. Delasalle	Thomas Pierrepoint	Henry Critchell
5 March 1946	Charles Prescott	Thomas Pierrepoint	Harry Kirk
26 March 1946	Arthur Charles	Stephen Wade	Harry B. Allen
13 December 1949	Benjamin Roberts	Stephen Wade	Harry Kirk
	John Wilson		Sydney Dernley
			Herbert Allen
11 July 1950	George Finlay Brown	Albert Pierrepoint	Harry Kirk
13 July 1950	John Walker	Stephen Wade	Harry Kirk
14 November 1950	Patrick Turnage	Stephen Wade	Sydney Dernley
21 March 1952	Tahir Ali	Stephen Wade	Harry Smith
24 December 1952	Herbert Appleby	Stephen Wade	Harry B. Allen
23 July 1957	John Willson Vickers	Harry B. Allen	Harry Smith
3 September 1958	Frank Stokes	Harry B. Allen	Harry Smith
17 December 1958	Brian Chandler	Robert Leslie Stewart	Thomas Cunliffe

INDEX

forthcoming titles in this series

Hanged at Pentonville

Hanged at Liverpool

Hanged at Manchester

other local titles

County Durham Strange But True

Robert Woodhouse

978-07509-3731-3

A fascinating book describing people, places and incidents that are unusual, odd or extraordinary. Discover the truth about flamboyant and eccentric characters, curious buildings, strange place names, weird weather, mazes, standing stones, holes in the ground and unusual customs.

Discovering County Durham & Teesside

Charlie Emett & Ron Dodsworth

978-07509-4670-4

100 of the most intriguing and historic sites in County Durham and Teesside are featured here – all accessible to the public. From landscape features to obscure villages, from remnants of forgotten industries to surprising buildings, all aspects of the area's history are included. *Discovering County Durham and Teesside* will be welcomed by anyone who is keen to know more about this remarkably varied part of Britain.